The Second Year

The Second Year

The Emergence of Self-Awareness

Jerome Kagan

With
Robin Mount
Susan Hiatt
Susan Linn
J. Steven Reznick
Charles L. Richman
Mary Maxwell Katz

Harvard University Press
Cambridge, Massachusetts, and London, England
1981

Library of Congress Cataloging in Publication Data

Kagan, Jerome.
   The second year.

   Includes bibliographical references and index.
    1. Self-perception in children.   2. Cognition in
children.   3. Infant psychology.   4. Nature and nurture.
I. Title.
BF723.S28K33   155.4'13   81–4214
ISBN 0–674–79662–4   AACR2

. . . For however each individual dreams,
it is through will alone
that future virtue is secured.

—Anonymous

Preface

Empirical study of the very young child, which has enjoyed a remarkable two decades of progress, has generally concentrated either
on the sensory and perceptual functioning of the infant under one
year of age or the growth of language in children between one and
three years. The nonlinguistic competences that appear soon after
the first birthday have been ignored, first, because of the absence of
persuasive theoretical statements regarding this era. Piagetian writings contain no phenomena in the second year that are as compelling
as the one-year-old's search for a hidden toy or the seven-year-old's
insistence on the conservation of the mass of a piece of clay. Trans-
formational grammarians have little to say about the growth of
memory, symbolism, or conscience during the second and third years,
and scientists committed to modern versions of psychoanalytic
theory remain more interested in the early bonding between infant
and mother than in the tensions that surround the acquisition of
standards.

Second, the small technical advances that have permitted new
generalizations about the infant's perceptual competences are less
appropriate for the two-year-old, who is too old to be treated as an
organism compelled to stare at high-contoured checkerboards but
still too young to tell stories, recall lists of words, or name tachisto-
scopically presented patterns. Thus investigators interested in the
second year of life are forced to rely on naturalistic observations and
experimental interventions that are closely tailored to the child's
everyday behavior and expectations. For these reasons, scientists attracted to this period tend to be friendly to inductive rather than
confirmatory investigations.

This monograph summarizes a group of related studies designed
to enhance understanding of the psychological changes that occur

during the second year. The work profits from the use of longitudinal designs and replication in different cultural settings, despite limited sample sizes and the temporary resistance of the explanations to elegant empirical test. It is hoped that this new information will generate deeper insight into what I and my colleagues have come to regard as a most significant developmental interval.

Many people contributed to the research reported in this monograph. Robin Mount, Susan Hiatt, and Susan Linn made the most substantial contribution to the gathering and analysis of the empirical data. Diana Lopez, J. Steven Reznick, Charles Richman, Mark Szpak, and Shirley Thompson were associated with the work throughout most of its implementation. Mary Maxwell Katz gathered the Fiji observations as part of her doctoral research. I directed the investigations and prepared the summary. I wish to thank Elizabeth Bates, Roger Brown, and Eve Clark for their many constructive comments on the manuscript, the staff of the Center for Advanced Study in the Behavioral Sciences for their technical support and generous mood, and Rebecca Low for her patience and care in preparing the final manuscript.

The empirical research was supported by funds from the National Institute of Child Health and Human Development, United States Public Health Service (Grant HD-10094), and the Foundation for Child Development. The preparation of the monograph, completed while the author was a Fellow of the Center for Advanced Study in the Behavioral Sciences, was supported by grants to the Center from both the National Science Foundation (BNS 78–24671) and the National Institute of Mental Health (2T32 MH14581–04).

JK

Contents

The Second Year

1

Classification of Children

There is a glaring disparity between the uniformity that characterizes the growth of young children and the variability that observers from different historical periods and cultures have imposed on their descriptions of these universal phenomena. Examples abound. All newborns with an intact central nervous system will tighten their tiny fingers around a pencil placed in their palms. Whereas nineteenth century observers were certain that this reaction was an early form of the adult proprietary instinct, modern observers who follow Piaget regard the same act as the initial structure in the growth of intelligence. These changes in the categories into which the phenomena of development are filed can be traced to altered presuppositions about human nature that are the inevitable product of the roll of history.

Explanations of the child's behavior during the last century adopted either a holistic or a mechanical frame. The former, popular with nineteenth century observers and central to Freudian theory, assumed that maturing functions, like will or ego, with the aid of experience, monitored the specific actions that comprised the child's behavioral surface. The spread of behaviorism and logical positivism after World War I provided a contrasting interpretive mode by analyzing the child into extremely specific, relatively independent dispositions that gradually became coherent through practice. This more mechanical model has dominated recent research in human development because of the increasing specialization among investigators and a proper concern with the empirical foundations of constructs. As a result, many developmental scientists have preferred to interpret their observations with concepts that remain close to the evidence and to avoid the ambiguous, overarching ideas that were so attractive to turn-of-the-century theorists.

Self-awareness is one of the nineteenth century ideas that has recently undergone renewed legitimization (Lewis and Brooks-Gunn, 1979). Although this term has no standard definition, most psychologists use it to refer to those processes that permit recognition of one's ability to act, to feel, and to regard self as an entity different from others. The return of this hypothetical function is due, in part, to the more permissive mood being generated by investigators in the cognitive sciences who have been forced by data to posit a host of central structures—such as schema and language acquisition device—that resist exact quantification but impose a coherence upon diverse behaviors. The processes that define the first phase of self-awareness appear to be inevitable products of maturation. Although awarding an enhanced role to the maturation of psychological functions necessarily implies a slightly diminished potency to social experience, even the most canalized competence requires an environmental context for its actualization. The song of the sparrow and the speech of the child will not appear without prior exposure to specific experiences, but they emerge with extraordinary regularity if the necessary events are present in the rearing environment. The more controversial suggestion is that self-awareness is a useful name for the pattern of behaviors that appear during the last part of the second year.

Category terms properly arouse debate because they imply the existence of events that have not been observed and contain a biased weighting of the facts. The datum contained in a one-year-old's building a tower of blocks was treated by Preyer (1888) as an exemplar of will; White (1959) called the same phenomenon an instance of the motive to be effective. The choice of one or the other of those abstract categories was the product of deep suppositions about human nature which during the opening decades of this century underwent a sudden change.

Authors of descriptive studies of psychological development rarely consider the premises that form the bases for their terminology. They typically choose descriptors and constructs that have gained consensual relevance and meaning from theory or from the concerns of their community, both of which have limited lives. The recent appearance of terms like *prosocial* and *androgyny* is due to a desire to emphasize the kind face of human nature and the new ethic surrounding relations between the sexes. Both terms are likely to be obsolescent by the turn of the century. A few, however, live longer than most because their connotations penetrate more deeply into the intuitions of a society. The *self, sense of self, self-awareness*, and *self-consciousness* belong to this more enduring set, at least in Western thought, because of the compelling belief that each of us can select acts and categorize our qualities. Although these ideas are fuzzy, they engage the most fundamental issues in developmental theory, including the contribution of maturation, the relation of the present to the future, and the mechanisms that permit growth to occur.

Scholars of the last century offered different resolutions to these issues and used different conceptual terms, because premises about human nature and its growth have not remained constant. The selection of names for the basic units in a domain of natural science has a serious influence on the development of theories and the rate at which that science moves toward coherence. Eighteenth century naturalists thought organs, not cells, were the basic structures; hence they had difficulty understanding how the original material contribution of the parents resulted in a fetus possessing all the structures necessary for life. Psychologists have assumed that will, motive, habit, conscience, and self have primary status and tried to trace the complexity of human behavior to these functions. But because human development is such a young discipline, its initial vocabulary, like the first words of the 2-year-old, contain words that are too broad or too vague for the events they are intended to summarize.

NB

The sentences used to describe and explain the behavior of children in the second year contain frequent references to self-awareness, maturation, continuity of growth, context of action, criteria of development, and the feeling state of uncertainty. Each of these ideas has a history, and it is useful to consider the fundamental themata which gave rise to them.

Classification Themes

The diversity among descriptions of the child's psychological characteristics can be organized around five different themes. The first concerns the balance between the biological inevitability of certain ① properties across extraordinarily varied environments and their dependence upon specific experiences. Although few societies believe that children possess no innate potentialities, cultures vary, over time and region, in the number of dispositions they are willing to award to nature, divinity, or fate. Nineteenth century observers of young children conceptualized their subject as a biological creature who inherited the potentiality for locomotion, imagery, language, memory, symbolism, reasoning, self-consciousness, and morality. Each of these characteristics would be actualized as long as the child grew in a world of objects and people. Maturation guaranteed that before the first year was over, children would begin to imitate adults; by the second year they would understand language; and by the third birthday they would know the difference between right and wrong—as long as

NATURE NURTURE

the environment supplied appropriate incentives, continued stimulus variety so that the child could use his discriminative abilities to create more articulated knowledge, and increases in pleasure and decreases in pain so that the profile of ideas and habits could be pruned to only the most adaptive attributes. Most nineteenth century theorists would have agreed with Maurice (1885) that in the human mind there is "a simple and primary idea of the distinction between right and wrong, not produced by experience but developing itself in proportion to the growth of the mind" (p. 80).

Although modern child psychologists are a little less willing to attribute that much power to biology, the few who do also recognize that genetically programmed attributes will not develop if children are isolated from all contact with an environment of changing events and symbolic communications from other people. Experience is always a necessary catalyst, even though in some cases its contribution can be minimal. Bühler (1930) reported that swaddled Albanian babies showed age-appropriate motor coordination soon after their bandages were removed, a finding analogous to Carmichael's (1927) demonstration that Ambystoma embryos, anaesthetized since hatching, swam at the same age as those who had spent their opening days under normal conditions.

A second organizing theme involves the duration of growth of an emergent function and the tension that comes from having to decide on the relative significance of early versus more recent antecedents of new behaviors. Many nineteenth century philosophers, historians, and natural scientists held that in order to understand any phenomenon, one had to have access to its entire history from origin to present—a position Mandelbaum (1971) called the bias of historicism. The nineteenth century historians who had rejected the mechanical view of man held by enlightenment philosophers took biology as the most informative model and likened the history of society to the growth of plants and animals. This frame assumes that any phenomenon that is part of a fixed sequence is a complex function of all that happened earlier. Each new stage grows out of the prior one, contains some of what went before, and moves inexorably toward a stage that is better than the one before. Tylor's (1878) view of the history of civilizations is prototypic: "It is indeed hardly too much to say that civilization, being a process of long and complex growth, can only be thoroughly understood when studied through its entire range; that the past is continually needed to explain the present, and the whole to explain the part" (p. 2).

The faith in a connectivity between the deep past and the present has been an essential premise in theories of development since the beginning of formal child study in the decades following Darwin. Theorists assumed a structural link between all phases of development and joined in affirmation of Russell's bold assertion that, "The chain of causation can be traced by the inquiring mind from any given point backward to the creation of the world" (in Hanson, 1961, p. 50). Many implied that no part of the child's past could ever be lost; every psychological property in the adult could, in theory, be traced to a distant origin. "If, then, from this law of habit there is no escape as long as we have bodies, if, by the time we are six years old, three-fourths of our actions are the result of habits formed; if, by the time we are grown up, 99 hundredths of our actions are so determined; if, in this way, our very life and destiny are dependent on the habits we form as we grow; then it follows that we cannot exaggerate the importance of the formation of right habits in childhood, neither can we exaggerate our own responsibility, as parents, in their formation" (Mumford, 1925, pp. 69–70).

Cf. "GRACE"

HABIT

Theorists influenced by Freudian ideas were bolder in their assertion of connectivity. Bernfeld (1929) asserted, "The powerful significance of the intellectual processes—perception, fantasy, thinking, and their social results in science, art, and philosophy in human beings—have their first roots in the specifically human mental structure of the three-month old child" (p. 138); "historically, all phenomena of adult mental life must be traceable to birth" (p. 213).

FREUD

Even textbook authors uncommitted to a particular theoretical view disseminated this catechism. Rand, Sweeny, and Vincent (1930) believed that the adult's sense of the aesthetic grows out of infant experiences: "General opinion agrees that aesthetic taste can be influenced even at such an early age. It is probably not desirable, then, to give him ugly toys which he may come to love because of the associations with them" (p. 260). Watson (1928) was the least equivocal: "At three years of age the child's whole emotional life plan has been laid down, his emotional disposition set" (p. 45).

DETERMINISM

Modern authors continue to proclaim their faith in this idea. "Variations in the early environment may exert profound effects on the individual's emotional and social development and possibly on intellectual development. The child's capacity for responding flexibly and adaptively to changing stimulus conditions, a necessity for proper development, may be impaired if his early experience is impoverished" (Hetherington and Parke, 1979, p. 153). Mussen, Conger, and Kagan (1969) suggested a connection between toilet training during the second year and later conformity: "Excessive timidity and over-conformity may also stem from unduly severe toilet training . . . Toilet training is a learned situation . . . in which the mother-child relationship may deteriorate, handicapping subsequent, healthy emotional and social adjustment" (p. 264–265).

The doctrine of connectivity implies a smooth, seamless continuity between new and old structures. James Mark Baldwin (1895) asserted that if a child repeats an act often enough, a new structure will form, for, "Every adaptation rises right out of the bosom of old processes and is filled with old matter" (p. 218). Piaget's (1951) interpretation of the rich and detailed descriptions of his own children's behaviors is also a celebration of connectivity: "Thus, when we studied the beginnings of intelligence we were forced to go as far back as the reflex in order to trace the cause of adapted schemas, for it is only by a principle of functional continuity that the indefinite variety of structures can be explained" (p. 6).

The premise of a connectivity is implied not only by asserting that dispositions shaped during the early years will be preserved but also, indirectly, by awarding to an infant's reaction a name that is appropriate for the adult—a frequent strategy in early textbooks on the child. Arlitt (1928) called the infant's tendency to stop crying when he is with a familiar person a sign of "gregariousness"; the tendency to cry when another baby does so is indicative of the instinct to "do as others do." Arlitt posited six instincts in the infant—self-assertion, to do as others do, to be uncomfortable at the sight of suffering, play, sex, and gregariousness—five of which are more applicable to older children and adults than to infants. These instincts did not strike Arlitt or her audience as odd because both she and her readers assumed a strong connectivity in development. Adult behavior has its origin in infancy; therefore, if one sees an early response that might be the origin of a later disposition, there is a strong tendency to assume that it is.

A third sign of the belief in connectivity is the awarding of primacy to the affects that appear early in development. Because crying (indicative of fear), motor discharge (indicative of rage), and babbling upon being touched (indicative of love) are seen during the first year, whereas signs of shame, guilt, and pride are not, Arlitt argued that the last three cannot be basic emotions. The doctrine of connectivity implies that whatever phenomena occur later in development must be derivatives of earlier processes.

This doctrine leads observers to view a custom, belief, or behavior in terms of its historical position rather than its function in the immediate present. Psychologists evaluate the behaviors indicative of an infant's attachment to a caretaker as a phase in the first year with both a history that begins at birth and an indefinite future. These behaviors are not transient phenomena. Historicism creates a consciousness which demands that the observer impose a judgment of the past and the future while watching an event that lasts only a few moments. A child who has spilled some glue on a valuable tablecloth runs to the mother and puts his lips to her cheek. Only with great difficulty can an observer view that event as an isolated "touching of lip to cheek." It requires enormous discipline to avoid ascribing to the child the private states that follow the spilling of the glue and the mother's receipt of the child's kiss. Those intrusions color the categorization of the event. The event, as it is happening now, is nothing in and of itself. Only its origin and consequences are of significance. In development, events take on an importance to the degree that the observer believes they make a contribution to the days to come. If they do not, they are often ignored.

Historicism appeals to Western scholars for several reasons. First, Western theories of cosmology have always been unusually curious about how and when life began. The story of Adam and Eve is known by all regardless of their religious affiliation. "As the twig is bent . . ." is an aphorism which has no contrasting maxim that awards as much potency to the present. More obviously, a philosophy of historicism is congruent with mechanism and a linear cause-effect epistemology. Each new event is best understood as occasioned by a temporally prior one; the temporally prior one occasioned by an event before that; and through such chained sequences the theorist proceeds linearly, gradually, and continuously to some original moment. For today's sunrise it was the origin of the universe; for the November election, it was the Pilgrims' landing at Plymouth Rock; for a June valedictorian speech, it was a particular adolescent's conception.

Historicism implies progress. Each new phase of change is more often than not better than the last, where *better* means more efficient, more humane, more rational, more moral, more powerful, more technical, more free, more virtuous—closer to perfection. Although the historian's faith in these assumptions began to fray by the end of the nineteenth century, that pessimism did not affect scholarship on human development. It is only during the last decade that some developmental scientists have come to question this philosophical attitude.

The major alternative to historicism does not deny the role of prior events but insists, first, that some new functions can have short rather than long histories and, second, that each novel phenomenon is dependent on a coherence of contemporary forces operating simultaneously. Although the first winter snowfall owes its appearance to a prior gradual change in the relation of sun to earth, there is additionally a host of local conditions that must occur if the flakes are to form. The child's first word requires a state of uncertainty or the motivation to communicate, as well as a history of exposure to language. Although the appearance of a new genetic mutation can have a history that is only a few seconds long, the Western mind has resisted the discontinuity implied in this class of event, for it spoils the aesthetic contained in the cumulative story. As a result, explanations of children's behaviors use terms that imply prolonged and gradual change.

The third determinant of classification terms for the child's psychological growth is a preference for constructs unconstrained by target or context, in contrast to categories that contain specific references to characteristics of the situation or the agent. Theorists who describe cognitive functioning, for example, have two extreme choices, neither of which is satisfactory. One strategy is to assume a single abstract process that monitors change and rate of growth in different competences over time. The velocity of growth of the abstract monitoring process is presumed to vary among children. In contemporary Western psychology this fuzzy idea gains clarity by being named "intelligence." The opposed view emphasizes separateness of function. The child possesses a large set of independent competences that emerge at different times and grow at different rates. The enhancement of each performance is monitored by its own special underlying ability, rather than by an overarching process that influences disparate talents.

Although the available facts fail to support either of these extreme positions, softer versions of each can be defended. The doctrine of a unitary mechanism is favored by the fact that most American children between 11 and 15 months of age display reliable imitation of others, symbolic play, and the comprehension of language. Despite the variety in the surface character of these displays, they emerge within a 4-month period, which implies, though it does not require, the postulation of a unitary process.

But there are many examples of independence among competences which appear early in development. Some children walk about one year before they begin to speak their first words; others play symbolically long before they are able to enter into a reciprocal relationship with another child. More important, most investigators have failed to find a correlation in healthy children between precocious or retarded development in any of the universal competences that appear between 12 and 18 months of age and precocity or retardation in the same or related capacities several years later. At the same time, studies of motivation and expectation have revealed how the hierarchy of motives is tightly yoked to particular contexts. The insight that children

and adults react to specific incentives with habits and ideas prefer- ?
entially linked to those incentives is relatively novel in child study; it
is not a rediscovery of an older position.

Until recently, Western scholars favored constructs that suppressed
the variety inherent in the interaction between person and situation.
Whether the constructs were will, consciousness, and intelligence, or
achievement, hostility, and anxiety, children were supposed to possess
potentials for action, intention, and feeling that generalized across
domains and persons. Once a child had will, she was supposed to
show this competence in all situations of choice. If a child were highly
intelligent, she would always benefit from experience and adapt better
than a child with less intelligence—no matter what the local perturba-
tion. Only during the last decade, as a result of the rich accumulation
of empirical data, have psychologists confronted the lack of correlation among cognitive performances that were thought to reflect the
same competence. For example, Sellers (1979) and Rogoff (1978)
found no relation between recall memory for different classes of
information. Moore, Kagan, and Sahl (in press) found no relation
between recall and recognition memory for words in either reading
disabled or normal subjects. These and other data have led Gelman
(1978) to suggest in a review of recent developmental research that
investigators accommodate to the specific demands inherent in each
problem situation.

The criteria for maturity comprise a fourth guide to classification
of psychological growth. Once philosophers, historians, and natural
scientists have selected a developing entity, they decide on the termi-
nus it seeks. Toynbee selected civilization; Hegel, objective spirit;
Comte, humanity. Nineteenth century psychologists picked character.
The child grew toward a more perfect morality, which was given an
absolute definition in the form of honesty, obedience, self-denial,
inhibition of aggression or anger, persistence, and hard work. Central
to these qualities was the ability to resist temptations to sexuality,
anger, selfishness, and idleness. These separate domains were not
independent; each contributed to an overarching morality. A flaw in
any one of them implied a defect in the whole. The ability to inhibit
temptation presupposed both a capacity for voluntary behavior, in
contrast to the involuntary instincts of the young infant, and an
awareness of right and wrong. Once the child knew the difference
between proper and improper behavior and was able to control his
actions, he could be held responsible for his behavior.

Although nineteenth century observers placed absolutely defined
character traits at the center of the ego ideal, by 1920 the definition of
maturity had become relative to local demands and could not be

specified for all children. Urban youngsters had to learn how to get along with unfamiliar peers; farm children had to learn their parents' skills. For those who attended school it was important to be above the median on tests of achievement, no matter what absolute level of skill the median represented.

When adjustment to the subculture replaced characterological qualities as the criterion for growth, it became more difficult to say of a particular child that she was immature or improperly trained. But the price of this tolerance was an unavoidable anxiety over not possessing the qualities of those who were better adjusted. Many nineteenth century children could reassure themselves of their virtue by obedience, honesty, and self-denial. They were capable of attaining at least one of the major defining properties of self-worth. But by the 1950s, when sin had become almost obsolescent, it was more difficult for the self to reassure itself of its essential goodness. Status, wealth, and friends, which were central parts of the definition of maturity, required a comparison with peers and a dependence on others for favors which would allow the individual to ascend in the rank that defined the self's position in relation to others. Hence, it was not as easy to award the self a pat-on-the-back whenever one chose.

The fifth and final organizational theme involves the hypothetical mechanisms invoked to explain how the infant becomes child, adolescent, and adult. Western theorists have relied primarily on three mechanisms to account for growth, with the balance among the three shifting across time. Biological maturation, the internalization of experience, and the relation between action and pleasure-pain are the only mechanisms employed by theorists with any regularity over the last two centuries. All observers wanted to know why the child acts, and they expected a purposive and mechanical answer. There was a deep resistance to the possibility that the energy involved in an action might be expended without some goal in the immediate present. An action did not mean a twitch of a limb or a brief facial grimace, but a coordinated action that appeared to be directed toward a goal and was terminated upon attaining that goal. Birds flew from one branch to another, babies kicked the sides of their cribs. Three answers were proposed: the child acts to maximize pleasure and minimize pain; the child acts in the service of habits established through conditioning or through the original operation of the pleasure-pain principle, which would include ideas and acts learned through observation; and the child acts because structures in the central nervous system have matured to permit the action to occur.

Although few theorists failed to declare loyalty to some form of the law of effect, most were faithful to Bentham and Locke in positing that the most significant consequences of an action were increases in pleasure and decreases in pain. Even Tiedemann (1787) was concerned with the agreeableness or disagreeableness of sensations and with the ideas that eventually developed from increasingly finer discriminations of agreeable or disagreeable experience. The pleasure and pain attached to experiences were key reasons for the growth of *Vorstellungen*. The centrality of pleasure was apparent in Tiedemann's interpretation of the first signs of animism in his child. Children, he maintained, attribute life to inanimate objects because inanimate objects are boring and do not provide agreeable sensations. Children attribute life to toys because that makes them more interesting and hence provides more pleasure.

Baldwin (1895) awarded pleasure and pain a central position in his explanation of how the child acquires new behavioral adaptations: "This process is . . . the neurological analogue of the hedonic consciousness; and the two aspects in which the happy variation shows itself in the consciousness of the higher organisms are pleasure and pain. These points may be summed up for discussion in the general proposition: the life history of organisms involves from the start the presence of the organic analogue of the hedonic consciousness . . . Pleasure accompanies normal psychophysical process, or its advancement by new stimulations which are vitally good; and . . . pain accompanies abnormal psychophysical process or the anticipation of its being brought about by new stimulations which are vitally bad" (pp. 176–177).

For Marwedel (1889) pain was the mechanism by which the sense of self emerged: "Before a child learns that the several members of its body are a part of itself, it must pass through many experiences, most of them more or less painful. My own child was 408 days old when, standing in its bed, it bit its own arm until it screamed" (p. 541).

The Freudian hypothesis of erogenous zones might be regarded as an extension of the pleasure-pain principle as an account of molar behavior to sensory functions. If actions followed by pleasure are repeated (the law of effect), and if the experiences of pleasure-pain are the primary bases for consciousness, then it is possible to extend the significance of pleasure to sensory function and to assume that taste, touch, sight, and hearing, though not skeletal, are also accompanied by pleasure. This idea is central to the concept of erogenous zones. Bernfeld (1929), who was strongly influenced by Freud, stated that the baby looks and listens in order to experience pleasure: "The eye is from birth very sensitive to light and moderate light stimuli release manifold reactions of pleasure: opening the eyes wide, turning the head toward objects, the breathing and pulse curves, are all more of the pleasure than of the pain type . . . No observer has neglected to mention the high pleasure tone, the great joy, and loud cooing of the child which occurred not only at the first seeing or during the first successful stage of the act of seeing, but which accompany seeing in general and which are especially gleeful and continuous during the first three months . . . the need to see is an instance of a general desire for pleasure. Because seeing brings pleasure it is exercised, and so intensely used, that it appears as if a need to see existed . . . thus, seeing is simply an activity, whose purpose is pleasure gain" (pp. 64, 68, 70).

Norsworthy and Whitley (1933) observed that humans continually want something and strive to satisfy wants and desires: "To describe what is meant by satisfying and annoying is difficult. Pleasure and pain with their usual connotations are not synonymous terms . . . Each tendency as it works itself out produces in the animal a feeling of satisfaction. In these feelings is found the original basis for all interests, motives, desires and wants—those things which control the life, activities, and education of the human race. In order to attain and preserve satisfying states and to avoid annoying states man is stimulated to learn" (pp. 43, 45).

The most recent textbooks regard the pleasure-pain principle as basic for attachment and moral development. Mussen, Conger, and Kagan (1974) stated that the states of discomfort experienced by the infant are "important psychologically for they force the infant to do something in order to alleviate the discomfort . . . Another person usually comes to tend the child when it cries or thrashes, and with this action the child's development comes under the partial control of the social environment" (p. 132). They argued further that, "The caretaking adult typically provides pleasant experiences and reduces the infant's pain and stress. As a result the infant becomes attached to its caretakers" (p. 227). Hetherington and Parke (1979) maintained that the child "is expected to learn these rules and to experience emotional discomfort or guilt when violating them and satisfaction when conforming to them" (p. 605).

But a small minority has continually disagreed with the majority opinion that pleasure-pain is the primary monitor of action. The eighteenth century philosopher Fichte, for example, rejected hedonism as the sole basis for behavior and insisted that man "is by nature a moral being—a being who is free and freely aspires to a constantly expanding sphere of activity" (in Mandelbaum, 1971, p. 218). Even Darwin (1871), who wanted to minimize the distance between humans and animals, rejected hedonism as the only mechanism for behavior: "In many cases, however, it is probable that instincts are followed from the mere force of inheritance without the stimulus of either pleasure or pain. A young pointer when it first scents game apparently cannot help pointing. A squirrel in a cage who pats the nuts which it cannot eat, as if to bury them in the ground, can hardly be thought thus either from pleasure or pain. Hence, the common assumption that men must be impelled to every action by experiencing some pleasure or pain may be erroneous" (I, 76). Thus, there has always been a tension between those who wish to ascribe development to the single hedonic principle and those who insist on adding biological maturation and observational learning to the list of mechanisms.

These five issues have influenced categorizations of the child. They may be summarized as involving the balance between nature and nurture, the past and the present, general and specific dispositions, absolute and relative criteria for development, and the significance of hedonic experience in psychological growth.

Shift after World War I

During the decade after World War I there was a major change in professional opinion on two of these five themes. Although the new cadre of child psychologists continued to favor general over specific constructs, historicism, and the centrality of pleasure-pain, the new group began to award to material social experience some of the formative power that had been assigned to hereditary potential, and they abandoned the absolute criteria of character for the relative criteria of adjustment to local societal demands. As a result, observers displayed an increasing tendency to describe the infant's interactive behavior with adults rather than her more solitary activities, to use motivation rather than will as a construct to explain action, and to assume that adjustment to society—which meant friends and material achievement—rather than character was the ideal toward which the child should move as she passed through the regular stages of development.

After 1920 it was not sufficient to state that the infant was able to discriminate spontaneously between hot and cold and to walk and speak meaningful language by two years of age. If the child's actions were not followed, and quickly, by certain events, especially reactions of other people, the child might never acquire the dipositions that most nineteenth century observers supposed to be inevitable. The nineteenth century view assumed that certain behaviors which characterized the human species must appear. The function of the pleasure-pain principle was to select those that would survive. The new view made the consequences of action the origin as well as the filter for the emerging behavioral profile. The influence of Darwinian theory, which had guaranteed a core set of human qualities, was almost completely lost. With the exception of Freud's first disciples, after 1920 the child was deprived of all but the most primitive instincts. Growth was the result of associating external events with feelings and actions.

The univocality of this assumption among American investigators became so strong that the eminent anthropologist Geoffrey Gorer (1955) was able to state unabashedly that a unified theory of social science rested on twelve postulates. The second postulate was: "Human behavior is predominantly learned. Although the human infant may be born with some instincts and is born with some basic drives whose satisfaction is necessary to its survival, it is the treatment which the infant undergoes from the other members of the society into which it is born and its experiences in its environment which are of importance in molding adult behavior" (p. 31). His fifth and sixth postulates were consistent with the second: "Habits are established by differential reward and puishment, chiefly meted out by other members of the society . . . The habits established early in life of the individual influence all subsequent learning, and, therefore, the experiences of early childhood are of predominant importance" (p. 32).

Although Locke (1690) had also argued that learning by association was a source of knowledge, he was particularly concerned with finding a material basis for moral ideas, and less motivated to explain memory, reasoning, sociability, emotional security, or freedom from neurosis. Locke's hidden agenda was different from that of Watson, Skinner, and Bowlby.

After World War I child psychologists became less interested in the development of those dispositions that would be part of every child's repertoire, and preoccupied with the differences among children in qualities that were not uniform to all, especially a sense of security and intellectual abilities. As a result, the learned products of social experience, especially encounters in the home, became the focus of theory and empirical study. Some modern theorists, such as Davis and Havighurst (1947), and Kagan (1979), emphasized not the raw interactive experiences seen by an observer but the child's private interpretations of that experience, but in both cases social experience was viewed as the incentive for change.

A striking index of the change is the amount of space that texts before and after World War I devoted to the family. Prior to 1910 it was rare for an author to devote more than a few paragraphs to the influence of the family on the child. After 1920 most texts devoted a lengthy section or entire chapters to parents, siblings, and the social class of the family as formative factors in the child's development.

Osofsky (1979) reserved three of the twenty-eight chapters in her *Handbook of Infant Development* to the effects of parent-child interaction on the abilities of the child, and none to the competences that might develop maturationally. The reasons were given by Huntington (1979), who asserted "We now know that what happens to infants and their families has an impact on life-long prevention of disability and the positive development of competence . . . The development of competence in very young children can be related from the earliest months onward to the interactions with their caregivers" (p. 840).

The replacement of character by adjustment as the index of mature development required definition of a term that was slippery because its defining characteristics changed with locale. By the 1930s most theorists implied that the term *adjusment* meant social skills, intellectual talent, emotional security, and a commitment to local values, each of which seemed to be the result of learning, not maturation. The layman's view of intellectual skills emphasized reading, writing, and arithmetic—talents that had to be taught to a child who wanted to master them. No child would be able to learn to multiply fractions spontaneously as he acquired speech or the capacity to empathize with the whine of shivering puppies.

Although nineteenth century observers believed the child inherited a basic disposition to obey—the child had "an innate disposition to follow precedent and rule, which precedes education" (Sully, 1896, p. 281)—by the 1940s most observers denied the child any special inclination to be socialized. The child was born with no unique tendencies to be moral; he had to be trained. The canon of pleasure-pain was consonant with the Freudian principle that the child wanted maternal love; hence, threat to or loss of maternal love, which became the modern exemplar of pain, became a primary incentive for adopting moral standards. "We are now able to summarize the motives which push the child to learn social controls. Certainly by the time the child is five or six years old, his desire to gain the approval of his parents is the chief motive for his accepting their cultural demands . . . The desire to win the social acceptance from his parents and older brothers and sisters (and very soon from his teachers and his playmates) becomes a major drive of his behavior. This drive is really a form of adaptive anxiety. It makes him anxious, first, to avoid punishment and, second, to win that approval which leads to social reward" (Davis and Havighurst, 1947, p. 38).

Merry and Merry (1950) stated: "In the final analysis it is social approval which asserts the strongest pressure upon the individual" (p. 223). Contemporary psychologists continued this theme. Mussen, Conger, and Kagan (1969) suggested, with respect to the mechanisms of socialization: "By the end of the first year, the child appears to be highly motivated to please parents and thus insure continued affection and acceptance and, in addition, and related to this, to avoid the unpleasant feelings generated by punishment or rejection . . . In a sense successful socialization involves an exchange in which the child gives up his desire to do as he pleases in return for the continued love and affection of his mother and father . . . Parental warmth and acceptance are necessary conditions for effective socialization" (p. 260).

All these writers were talking about the same mundane set of events. The child washes his hands before dinner, brushes his teeth before bedtime, and refrains from swearing when angry, throwing a plate at the wall, or hitting his younger brother. It is not obvious that the reliability of these inhibitions is traceable to, and only maintained by, fear of the loss of love. Two-year-olds are affectively bothered by a great many events whose central dimension is the fact that the integrity of an object has been violated. It is possible that the child's affective distress to these events is not due only to a fear of loss of love, and that nineteenth century theorists may have been correct when they hypothesized a built-in moral sense.

What historical events in the larger society permitted these changes in perspective and classification to occur so quickly? Why did it take less than twenty years for Pavlovian and Freudian ideas to enter American books, but almost forty years for Piagetian theory to become as popular? It is reasonable to assume that American child psychologists, and many educated American citizens, were prepared to believe that the learned products of parental interactions with children, especially the mother's restrictiveness and affection, were of profound significance for development. Of the many events during the second and third decades of the twentieth century that could have contributed to the dramatic shift from a concern with the maturation of absolute character to a preoccupation with individual differences in adjustment acquired through experience, four seem to have special significance: the increased prejudice against European immigrants, the results of the standardized IQ testing performed on recruits during World War I, the desire of psychologists to argue from scientific evidence, and the celebration of relativism.

During the years before World War I, there was a serious increase in racial and ethnic tension between the new European immigrants and urban black populations, on the one hand, and the Caucasian majority, on the other. May (1959), among others, documented that the increase in European immigration and the enlargement of poor black neighborhoods in the cities produced increased suspicion and hostility between middle-class whites and the minority groups, as well as legislation restricting immigration. This strife was especially strong during the mid-1920s: "Part of the reason for increasing tension was, as in earlier crises, economic. The depression of 1914 revived labor's fears of foreign competition and decreased the employer's interest in a steady flow of immigrant workers. And everytime anybody, for any reason, worried about the preservation of old ways, he was likely to glance with alarm, at the annual inflow of half a million newcomers" (p. 347).

The prejudice was maintained in part by the popular assumption that the differences in ability, status, character, and criminality between native and immigrant groups were essentially biological in origin. The bias against blacks was then, as now, centered on intellect. Ferguson (1916) put the bias in statistical terms: "Pure negroes, negroes three-fourths pure, mulattoes, and quadroons have roughly 60, 70, 80 and 90 percent respectively of white intellectual efficiency" (p. 125).

The belief that ethnic differences in habits, styles of interaction, and especially mental ability were genetic was strengthened when the mental tests administered to recruits upon America's entry into World War I revealed that the blacks and ethnic minorities had the lowest scores. Robert Yerkes (1921) and Lewis Terman (1916), two of the most influential psychologists of the time, suggested that differences in ability might be under partial genetic control. Because these objective scores were regarded as an index of biological qualities, they forced many Americans to confront an idea that was threatening to the national egalitarian ethos. I suggest that a large proportion of educated Americans with a liberal philosophy wanted to believe in the ideal of a society in which poor and disadvantaged could, through effort and education, lift themselves to the middle class. May (1959) affirmed the validity of this hypothesis: "The first and central article of faith in the national credo was, as it always had been, the reality, certainty, and eternity of moral values" (p. 9). In this moral scheme evil "was incarnate in extreme inequality, political corruption and ruthless power" (p. 22). Thus, the mental test scores represented a serious inconsistency in national philosophy. If poor immigrant Italians, Irish, and Jews were biologically less talented than native Caucasians, individual effort and proper education might not work. The resulting dissonance may have been as serious a source of unease as the most recent writings of Konrad Lorenz and E. O. Wilson, which implied that moral attitudes toward aggression should be based on evolutionary facts, or Skinner's claim that the individual is not free because each action is the determined product of past conditioning. The educated liberal, then as now, was eager for any weapon that would neutralize the racial inferiority hypothesis.

But for psychologists trained after 1910, the defense of egalitarianism had to be rational and empirical, for psychology was trying to define itself as an independent, experimental natural science, distinct from philosophy and biology and pruned of metaphysics. Hence, the critique of racial inferiority had to be based on scientific evidence. Pavlov's work, which had been made popular by John Watson, was seized upon by the new cadre of psychologists. Conditioning was elegant, experimental, and distinctly psychological. Its subject matter and concepts, such as stimuli, responses, and reinforcements, were not familiar to biology, anthropology, or philosophy. They belonged uniquely to the new scientific profession of psychology. Additionally, conditioning emphasized the role of experience, not biology, in promoting both change and stability of psychological attributes. By the late 1920s, conditioning had become a key mechanism in development, and experience in the family had become the main occasion for learning new dispositions. Whether Watson and his colleagues realized it or not, by emphasizing the powerful role of conditioning, they were supplying the intellectual weapons necessary to defuse the racial inferiority hypothesis. By the 1930s the battle was over. The hypothesis of innate racial inferiority was essentially discarded, even though the data affirming the influence of genetics on mental traits had become slightly stronger. These ideas were accepted so quickly because there was a fire to put out, namely the threat to society implied by the hypothesis of racial inferiority.

A fourth ingredient in the transition to an experiential basis for growth was the relativism inherent in the criterion of adjustment. The philosophy of pragmatism had been growing for the two decades since James borrowed and popularized Peirce's more abstruse views. The principle that actions and decisions were local to situations gradually became part of normative philosophy. What suits the situation best was to be the criterion for the morally proper decision. "Morality was no longer a fixed unchanging code . . . People no longer needed the old fixities; they could do better without them (and few doubted, at bottom, that they knew what better meant). Repudiate, commanded a generation of relativist thinkers, the outworn notions of universal moral absolutes. When this is done, we will be able to advance toward truth, freedom, and justice" (May, 1959, p. 141).

World War I added some necessary skepticism. The innocence implied in the pietistic views of Howells, Taft, and other turn-of-the-century Americans was shattered with the war. If the world was irredeemably evil, the only reasonable life strategy was to determine what was required and get it. Successful adaptation—getting what was required—defined virtue. If there was no absolute attribute that all children must acquire, but rather each child should develop whatever talents and values fit his time and location, then individual variation in the attainment of the local good became more interesting than the growth of the species toward some hypothetical terminal state that may not exist. Thus, psychologists turned to the problem of individual variation in adjustment: how to predict it from behavioral signs in early childhood, its correlated background factors, and ways to intervene in order to hasten it.

Analogous historical processes occurred during the 1970s. The environmental intepretation of adjustment, which grew steadily more popular, reached a crest in the 1950s when even extreme forms of psychopathology, like schizophrenia and autism, were regarded as totally environmental in origin. Following the civil rights movement and the desegregation of schools, society was led to believe that sufficient expenditure of money and effort to improve the education of minority children would alleviate the gap in wealth and occupational status between the classes. Unfortunately it did not. This apparent failure, like the test scores five decades earlier, had to be confronted and reconciled with the unswerving belief in environmentalism. Additionally, scientists found that schizophrenia had a genetic component and autism was not simply the product of a harsh mother. The philosophy of extreme environmentalism suddenly became vulnerable at a time when biology was having extraordinary success in demonstrating the brain's inherent properties, including the way the brain responds to stimuli and the effect of neurotransmitters on mood and action. Hence, biological explanations of behavior met as receptive an audience as conditioning theory did a half-century earlier, for it seemed to provide a rational explanation for the failings in the adjustment of minority groups. But the outcry was strong from those who still believed in the egalitarian ethic. Some of the current arguments against sociobiology often reduce to statements of faith in egalitarianism.

Study of the Second Year

Naturalistic investigations of the young child are producing support for the nineteenth century belief that many of the significant characteristics of the opening years mature in an orderly fashion as long as children encounter people and objects. The reconsideration of this premise owes some of its vitality to a more inductive and less confirmatory approach to study of the infant. In earlier work my colleagues and I assumed the reality and theoretical utility of general constructs like passivity, sociability, hostility, achievement, reflectivity, and identification, and made our observations accommodate to those ideas (Kagan and Moss, 1962; Kagan, 1971). Although these concepts seemed useful in integrating both naturalistic and experimental observations with older children, they were less appropriate to the behavioral repertoire of the infant. Gradually, almost unconsciously, I began to shift my empirical strategy and accommodate to the typical surface behaviors of the young child. During the first year infants look, smile, and babble to stimuli, play with objects, and show imitation or distress at the unexpected and the unfamiliar. I noted the developmental course of these behaviors in relation to varied classes of incentives and, after discovering regularities, invented constructs like the discrepancy principle and enhanced retrieval capacity, consciously resisting the use of constructs that implied a theoretical similarity to the behaviors of older children or adults (Kagan, Kearsley, and Zelazo, 1978; Kagan, 1979a and b).

It seemed reasonable to extend this Baconian attitude to study of the second year of life. We began these studies without any overarching theoretical conception of the major milestones between 12 and 24 months of age. Piagetian theory is not a particularly useful guide to this era, and systematic research on this period is still sparse. But no investigator ever begins his work without prejudice. The selection of variables is the first demand of science, and selection always implies *a priori* ideas. The tasks we chose and the behaviors we selected for quantification were influenced by a central supposition about early development, namely, that the emergence of cognitive competences resulting from the maturation of the central nervous system in children living with people and objects is essential to understanding the changing profile of behavior during the early years. Retrieval memory, the generation of plans, and inference are requisite for the universal fear of strangers and of separation from the caretaker and for the modal patterns of interaction with adults, children, and objects. We therefore selected experimental procedures that emphasized these cognitive functions.

Although maturation of the central nervous system also makes a substantial contribution to the development of both motor coordination and affect, we concentrated on cognitive functions because progress in science is most likely to occur when the state of knowledge surrounding the phenomenon is relatively rich and the functional relation chosen for inquiry seems to invite solution. The relation between maturation of the brain and growth of cognitive functions is, at the moment, a bit more amenable to empirical investigation than the comparable relation between maturation and motivational or social phenomena. This is an historical, not an epistemological, defense of the content of this investigation.

But lest I raise hopes for promises I cannot keep, this is not a study of the relation between brain growth and behavioral development. Specification of the biological changes that accompany a child's altered psychological profile cannot be written in this decade. However, the meager information available on ontogenetic changes in myelinization, neuron density, and patterns of electrical discharge suggests parallels with psychological functioning. If these concordances are not coincidences, future investigators will be able to write the prose that removes some of the mystery from these associations.

The history of developmental psychology contains a guide for the choice of variables and procedures. The study of behaviors that dominate the repertoire during a particular phase of development often leads to inferences about process that are occasionally concealed when the reactions to experimental procedures are assessed, if the situations require responses less natural to that developmental stage. Brown's (1973) list of the sequence of morphemes mastered during the early stage of speech development provides a productive example of the inductive mode, in contrast with the Breland and Breland (1960) description of the difficulty of teaching animals responses that are not part of their natural capacity. Even if one is successful, the response may vanish spontaneously.

Young children are uncertain in most experimental situations, and this state is often a major cause of their reactions. Thus, we devoted a great deal of time to observing behaviors that are prominent during the second year in the familiar home setting with the mother present. These included play with toys, imitation, speech, and social interaction. The explicit assumption was that these are universal behaviors whose time of appearance reflects the rate of maturation of more basic psychological functions, just as the age of appearance of pubic and axillary hair indexes the time when important changes are occurring in the hypothalamus, pituitary, and gonads. Indeed, the changes of puberty provide a useful model for our work. As reproductive fertility is established, there are surface changes in the distribution of hair, size of the genitals, pitch of voice in males, and breast size in females. It is not obvious that these diverse phenomena have their origin in an endocrine mechanism that is triggered by an alteration in hypothalamic sensitivity to circulating sex hormone.

We evaluated five classes of behavior that emerge during the second year. The first is intelligible speech. During the second year most children replace unintelligible phonemic combinations, many of which are selective and nonrandom, with one- and two-word utterances typically descriptive of events in the child's immediate environment and of the child's moods, desires, and actions.

A second class of behavior arising in the child's second year which we studied is concern with parental prohibitions and violations of parental standards. The child in the second year reveals a preoccupation with objects that are broken, incomplete, dirty, or out of place, and with aspects of his toilet training.

The third phenomenon is the enhanced quality of performance on tasks set by adults, the avoidance of tasks that are too difficult to master or implement, and the seeking of challenging activities. These behaviors suggest that the child has generated some awareness of her talents and, as White (1959) noted, wants to be instrumentally effective. One of our children said, "Do it self," as she pushed away her mother who was trying to help her daughter climb up on a chair.

Social interaction is the fourth class of response we evaluated. The appearance of reciprocal play with another child and sustained dialogue with an adult imply the capacity, albeit limited, to understand the intentions of another and to anticipate her actions.

And finally, appreciation of the difference between pretense and reality appears during this interval. The 2-year-old will conduct imaginary conversations on the telephone and whisper softly, "Shh, shh," as she puts a doll to sleep. The verbally precocious child may even say to her mother, "Tend it's a baby."

These five new talents are obviously different from one another in their surface form. But the appearance of these functions becomes more reasonable if one posits, as nineteenth century observers did, that during the last half of the second year children become aware of their actions, intentions, and competences and try to accommodate their behavior to the standards they are generating or have acquired. I suggest as a tentative hypothesis that children indeed seem to become self-conscious during this 6-month era. It would have been difficult during most of the last half-century for a psychologist interested in infancy to decide *a priori* to study the ontogeny of self-awareness, even though that idea had been popular a hundred years earlier.

Although we imposed the name *self-awareness* on some of the coherences we uncovered, that name is not an explanation of the phenomena; it is only a way to convey a guess as to the nature of the underlying processes. We used a word rather than a number or alphabetical letter because the connotations of the label direct future studies. When Moruzzi and Magoun (1949) detected a lawful relation between the reactivity of neurons in the reticular activating system and both the behavioral states of the animal and their imposed stimulation, they elected to call the coherence "arousal." The word did not explain the data but conveyed their untested belief that future research would reveal that the reticular activating system is a vital participant in the organism's propensity to action. When Spemann and Mangold (1924) observed that transplantation at early gastrulation of the dorsal lip of the blastopore of one embryo (the newt *triton cristatus*) into the ectoderm of another embryo (*triton taenitus*) produces a new embryonic axis, they needed a name for the effect of the transplanted tissue. They chose "organiser." The word is not an explanation of the remarkable set of events, but does possess important connotations.

Our research passed through three stages. During the first we followed two cohorts of children of different ages for about 10 months, studying play, memory, the child's reaction to modeling, transposition, and interaction with a peer. This investigation revealed two facts of importance. First, there was a major change in cognitive performance around the second birthday. Second and more significant was the display of distress after the 20- to 23-month-old child saw a moderately familiar person model some acts in front of the attentive youngster. The need to understand this phenomenon more deeply led to the second phase of the project, which involved the study of two cross-sectional samples of children in order to eliminate alternative interpretations of this event. Reflection on these results suggested that during the latter half of the second year children seemed to be becoming aware of standards for behavior and of their competence to meet them. The need for a richer corpus to clarify these musings led to the final studies, one of which was a detailed examination of the growth of six children who were followed for close to 10 months in their homes.

The changes observed in the months prior to the second birthday can be understood by assuming the emergence of three related competences: an awareness of those actions and events that violate standards, an awareness of the ability or lack of ability to meet standards imposed by the self and others, and an awareness of one's own actions. Although these functions are not identical, they seem to involve standards and the recognition of one's ability to meet them. These constructs are inductive ideas imposed after the data were gathered; they did not provide the guiding intellectual impetus for the work.

2

Sources of Evidence

Study 1

The purpose of the first investigation was to determine the growth functions and interrelations for a selected set of behaviors that seemed to rest on emerging cognitive competences. The behaviors chosen were symbolic play, imitation, speech, relational and linguistic inference, memory for location, drawing a face, and patterns of social interaction with a peer. It was decided to assess two small longitudinal samples frequently rather than larger cross-sectional groups because of both the increasing rapport that is the dividend of repeated evaluations of the same child and the belief that it would be easier to detect transitions with longitudinal than with cross-sectional data.

One sample of fourteen younger children (seven boys and seven girl, thirteen firstborn and one later born) was observed monthly from 13 to 22 months. This sample is referred to as the younger cohort. Six children in this group were seen additionally at 26, 27, 28, and 30 months. The sixteen children in the older cohort (eight boys and eight girls, eleven firstborn and five later born) were seen monthly from 20 to 26 months; fifteen of these children were seen monthly from 20 to 29 months and again at 30, 32, and 34 months. All thirty children in this longitudinal study were Caucasian and middle class (see Table 2.1).

The subjects were recruited through birth records from local hospitals and newspaper advertisements in the Cambridge metropolitan area. One month before the formal assessments began, when the children were 12 and 19 months of age, pairs of subjects came to the laboratory with their mothers in order to become familiar with the testing environment and the child with whom they had been matched by sex and age for future play sessions. Both children were

Table 2.1. Demographic characteristics of longitudinal samples (Study 1).

| | Mean years | | | | | |
| | Mother | | Father | | Mother and father | |
Subject	Education	Age	Education	Age	Education	Age
	Older cohort					
Girl	14.6	30.4	16.3	33.3	15.4	31.8
Boy	15.5	30.7	16.9	31.9	16.2	31.3
Total	15.1	30.6	16.6	32.6	15.8	31.6
	Younger cohort					
Girl	16.6	28.3	17.7	28.9	17.1	28.6
Boy	14.4	27.0	15.0	30.3	14.7	28.7
Total	15.5	27.6	16.4	29.6	15.9	28.6

part of the longitudinal sample. Each month thereafter the child came to the laboratory on two separate days, each visit typically separated by a day or two. The sequence of procedures was constant for all children for the two sessions every month.

On the first visit to the laboratory, the five procedures administered were relational inference, symbolic play, imitation of a model, linguistic inference, and memory for location.

Relational inference. The purpose of this procedure was to determine if the subjects could "relate" their knowledge of the differential size of infants and adults to the weights of inanimate objects by asking the child to identify a "daddy" and a "baby" from two identical yellow ping-pong balls of the same size but of different weights. The heavier one (the daddy) weighed 27.7 gm, while the lighter one (the baby) weighed 1.7 gm.

The child was presented with the two balls simultaneously, one in each hand. Upon giving the balls to the child, the experimenter said, "I have a daddy and a baby. Can you give me the daddy?" Each child received four trials each month, two on each monthly visit to the laboratory. The hand that received the heavier ball and the name of the person asked for varied with each presentation. Testing terminated when the child correctly identified the balls on four consecutive trials, that is, when the child gave the heavier ball for the adult on two occasions and the lighter ball for the baby on two occasions.

Symbolic play. A 20-minute symbolic play session was conducted on each of the two visits every month, during which the duration and quality of all play with objects and the child's spontaneous utterances were recorded. During the first visit of each month, the toys were realistic representations of familiar objects. On the second visit, the toys were nonrealistic and included blocks, pieces of cloth, and plastic rings. For the older cohort the toy sets were combined at 27–32 months.

After 10 minutes of play, and on a signal from the second observer in the adjacent control room, the examiner and mother joined the child on the floor. The examiner then modeled three different acts with appropriate verbalizations. She repeated each act slowly, making sure the child, who was seated on the mother's lap, was watching. The acts modeled, which became more complex as the child matured, were:

Age (mos.)	Younger cohort
13–16	1. Feed bottle to zebra.
	2. Put doll in bed.
	3. Wash doll's face with washcloth.
17–21	1. Make doll talk on telephone.
	2. Make doll ride a horse.
	3. Put hat on a pig.
22	1. Make doll talk on telephone.
	2. Make doll cook banana in pan and have two dolls eat dinner on two plates.
	3. Make three animals walk, simulate rain by hand motions, and have animals hide under a cloth to avoid getting wet.
	Older cohort
20–21	Same acts as for younger cohort, 13–16 months of age.
22–26	Same acts as for younger cohort, 22 months.
27–29	Make three dolls throw a ball of yarn back and forth among them (only one act was modeled at these ages).

After the experimenter modeled the appropriate acts, she merely said, "Now it's your turn to play." She did not request the child to imitate her actions. The child was then allowed to play for an additional 10 minutes.

Durations of nonsymbolic and symbolic play were recorded by one observer on an event recorder located in an adjacent room. The second observer dictated a description of the child's behavior into a tape-recorder which was simultaneously recording the child's speech through microphones attached to the ceiling of the room. Additionally, the observer in the room with the child and mother wrote down all of the child's utterances verbatim. These records were used to code symbolic play with toys, behavior following the model's actions, and a number of linguistic variables.

Linguistic inference. The purpose of this procedure was to determine if the child would infer that an unfamiliar linguistic term referred to an unfamiliar object. The child was seated at a table facing the experimenter. The experimenter first presented the child with a trio of known objects (a toy cat, car, and cup). After allowing the child to play with the toys for approximately one minute, the experimenter asked the child to hand her the cat, then the car, then the cup, in three separate questions. If the child gave the wrong object to the experimenter or failed to respond, testing was terminated. If the child correctly identified all objects, that is, gave the object requested, the experimenter proceeded to the critical test trial. The experimenter placed two namable objects (a doll and dog) and one unfamiliar object that had no name (either a wooden or styrofoam form) in front of the child. After allowing the child to play with these items, the experimenter then said, "Give me the zoob (or iboon)." The nonsense syllable used alternated from month to month. After asking the child for either the zoob or the iboon, the experimenter asked the child to hand her the dog and the doll. When the child correctly gave the unfamiliar shape following the request for the nonsense word, testing ended. All responses were coded by the observer in the adjacent room.

Memory for location. The purpose of this procedure was to assess the child's ability to recall the location of a prize when the number of interfering elements and delay were varied systematically. The child was brought into a different room adjacent to the playroom and introduced to the apparatus, which consisted of a screen and a table. The child was seated on the mother's lap facing the experimenter and next to a stage on which the materials could be presented. The child was shown either a raisin or a Cheerio. Depending upon the child's preference, one was used as the prize the child was to find under one of several receptacles. The child watched the examiner hide the prize under one of the receptacles, the receptacles were screened for a delay, the screen was lifted, and the examiner asked the child to find the prize. Initially the child was introduced to the apparatus using only one receptacle and no screen. A screen was then added. After the child understood the task and could successfully reach for the correct receptacle after it had been screened with a one-second delay, the test series began.

The child was first tested under one-second delays with an opaque screen lowered during the delay. Under the one-second delay condition the child was tested using two, four, six, or eight receptacles, each of a different color, shape, and size. The testing always followed the same order. The child was first presented with two different receptacles. If she found the reward on two consecutive trials with a one-second delay, the experimenter proceeded to six containers. If the child was successful with six containers and a one-second delay, the experimenter proceeded to eight receptacles. If the child failed to find the reward with six receptacles the experimenter reduced them to four. If the child was not correct with four receptacles, testing was terminated for that month. If the child found a reward with eight receptacles and a one-second delay, the experimenter repeated the procedure with a 5-second delay, beginning with two containers and following the same procedure through eight containers. If the child was successful with a 5-second delay the experimenter repeated the procedure with a 10-second delay for two, six, and eight receptacles.

A total of ten receptacles of different sizes and colors were used for testing. The reward was never hidden in the same location twice in succession. Additionally the receptacle that hid the reward on a particular trial was removed from the series and not used on the next trial. This was done in order to prevent the child from associating a particular receptacle with the reward. When the child found the reward with eight different receptacles and a 10-second delay, the entire procedure was readministered using identical containers (a set of green cups of the same size and color).

Testing continued until the child failed a particular item twice or until the child became too restless or irritable to proceed. When the child returned the following month, after she was again familiarized with the apparatus, testing began with the last item that the child had solved correctly the previous month. When the child found the prize with eight identical receptacles and a 10-second delay, testing terminated. The child's responses were recorded by an observer located in the adjacent control room, who observed the testing through a one-way mirror. Each of the test items was given a score according to a scheme based on the number of receptacles and the delay. When the receptacles were different, the scoring scheme was:

No. receptacles	Delay (secs.)	Score
2	1	1
4	1	2
6	1	3
8	1	4
2	5	5
4	5	6
6	5	7
8	5	8
2	10	9
4	10	10
6	10	11
8	10	12

When the receptacles were identical, the scoring scheme was:

No. receptacles	Delay (secs.)	Score
2	1	13
4	1	14
6	1	15
8	1	16
2	5	17
4	5	18
6	5	19
8	5	20
2	10	21
4	10	22
6	10	23
8	10	24

On the second visit to the laboratory, or Session 2, the child was first administered the relational inference test, as in Session 1, and then the symbolic play procedure with nonrealistic toys. These two procedures were followed by three new tests: drawing a face, transposition, and peer play.

Drawing a face. In this procedure the child first watched the examiner draw a schematic face, which consisted of a circle containing two dots for eyes, a vertical line for the nose, and a curved line for the mouth. The child was then given a crayon and paper and asked to draw the face while the model remained in view.

Transposition. The purpose of this procedure was to determine if the child could relate his or her knowledge of the relative differences in size between adults and children to inanimate objects that varied in size. The child was asked to identify a "daddy" and a "baby" from two wooden squares that varied in size. The child was seated at a table facing the experimenter. The stimuli used were wooden squares, painted flesh color and measuring 0.5, 1.0, 1.5, 2.0, 2.5, and 3.0 dm. There were two phases to the transposition procedure—near and far.

In near transposition, the child was shown the 1.5 and 2.0 dm squares on four separate trials with position counterbalanced. The experimenter said, "I have a daddy and a baby. Which one is the baby?" If the child identified correctly the 1.5 dm square as the baby on three of four trials, the fifth trial was presented. On the fifth trial, the child was shown 1.0 and 1.5 dm squares, with the 1.0 dm square presented to the left, and asked, "Which one is the baby?"

The same procedure was followed with the 1.5 and 2.0 dm squares, but now the experimenter asked, "Which one is the daddy?" If the child correctly identified the 2.0 square as the daddy on three of four trials, the fifth trial was presented. It consisted of 2.0 and 2.5 dm squares, with the 2.5 dm square presented to the child's left and the experimenter asking for the daddy.

After each correct response the experimenter rewarded the child by saying, "That's right." If the child was unable to complete the near transposition phase of testing, the session was terminated and testing resumed the following month. If the child was able to complete the first phase of the task, the following month the child was tested for far transposition.

In far transposition, the child was first presented with a 1.5 dm and 2.0 dm square, and the experimenter said, "I have a daddy and a baby. Which one is the baby?" If the child correctly identified the 1.5 dm square as the baby three out of four times, the fifth trial was presented. It consisted of presenting 0.5 and 1.0 dm squares, and the experimenter asked, "Which one is the baby?"

This procedure was repeated with the 1.5 and 2.0 dm squares. However, this time the experimenter asked, "Which one is the daddy?" If the child correctly identified the 2.0 dm square as the daddy on three out of four trials, the fifth trial was presented. It consisted of 2.5 and 3.0 dm squares, about which the experimenter asked, "Which one is the daddy?" If the child was unable to complete the far transposition phase of testing, the session was terminated, and testing resumed the following month. The child's responses were recorded by the observer in the adjacent room.

Peer play. In order to observe developmental changes in social interaction, a 20-minute peer play session was conducted in the same room where the earlier play session had occurred. Each child was matched on sex and age with another child who was also a subject in the study. All peer play sessions were conducted with the same pairs of children.

The children were brought into the playroom by their mothers and allowed to play with one of two sets of appropriate toys. The toys were different from the ones used in the symbolic play sessions, and toy sets were alternated each month. Each set of toys had several objects conducive to social play (telephones, a puzzle box, a tea set). The two mothers remained seated on the couch during the play session and were instructed not to initiate any action or encourage the children to play together. They were encouraged to intervene only if the play became rough or if their child approached them for comforting.

The duration of each child's solitary play, symbolic play, and reciprocal or parallel interactions were recorded on a continuous chart recorder by two observers located in an adjacent control room. A third observer dictated the activities of each child into a tape-recorder. This recording was used to code the frequency of occurrence of offering objects to the peer, imitating the peer's behavior, and aggression against the peer.

The children were scheduled so that on one monthly visit the peer play session was the last procedure administered; on the following month the peer play was the first procedure. This schedule was followed so that every other month each child would have an opportunity to play when he or she was most alert.

Study 2

The most surprising finding in Study 1 was the occurrence of behavioral signs of anxiety following the model's actions during the symbolic play sessions. It appeared that this display of distress might be interpreted as reflecting the child's awareness of his inability to duplicate the model's responses. In order to control for alternative explanations of the children's reactions to the modeled acts, Studies 2 and 3 were implemented.

The most likely alternative was that the distress occurred because the model interrupted the child's play. Thus in Studies 2 and 3 observations were made of the child's reactions after the adult simply rearranged the toys rather than modeling any coherent action. Additionally, in Study 2 the effect of the familiarity of the model was evaluated by having the mother display the same acts that the examiner performed in Study 1.

In Study 2, the subjects were forty-nine children from the Cambridge area, 22 to 23 months of age, who were seen for one session. The mother and the female examiner (that is, the model) sat on the couch, while the child was allowed to play for 10 minutes with the same set of realistic toys used with the longitudinal cohorts in Study 1. The children were divided at random into three groups. At the end of the 10 minutes of play one of three different events occurred, depending on the group to which the child had been assigned.

In Group 1 (n = 19) the examiner came to the child, sat down on the floor, and said she was going to play with the toys. She then gently rearranged the toys for about 2 minutes, which approximates the time taken to model the three acts, but she did not implement any coherent actions with the toys. The examiner then returned to the couch to talk to the mother. In Group 2 (n = 18) the same examiner modeled the three acts that were displayed with the longitudinal children at 22 months of age (telephone to the doll's ear, cooking sequence, animals walking in the rain). As in that study, the examiner did not tell the child to display the acts after they had been modeled. She merely said to the child, "Now it's your turn to play." In Group 3 (n = 12) the mother came to the child and, in accord with previous instructions, modeled the same three acts that had been demonstrated by the less familiar examiner in Group 2 with the same verbal comments. An observer located behind a one-way vision screen coded all behavioral signs of distress, such as fretting, crying, clinging to the mother, and requests to go home.

Study 3

The subjects of Study 3 were forty-eight children, half of them 18 months old and the other half 24 months old, with both sexes equally represented. All children came from middle-class families living in Winston-Salem, North Carolina, whose average annual income was $25,000 and average level of education was 16.2 years.

Each infant visited a laboratory at Wake Forest University twice, with an intersession interval of two days. Subsequent to assessments of the cognitive functioning of the child, the mother and the model accompanied the child into the room. After 10 minutes of free play with the toys, the infant was directed to watch the model play while the infant sat on the mother's lap.

For half the children, the model played with the objects in a random manner in the first session, modeling no acts. In the second session, she modeled three different acts. For the remaining half of the sample, the modeling of the three acts occurred in the first session and the random sorting in the second. The random sorting consisted of the model picking up three different toys, shuffling them on the floor, and repeating this behavior two more times with two different sets of objects. The acts modeled for the 18-month-olds were the same three acts used with the 17- to 21-month-old infants in Study 1. The acts modeled for the 24-month-olds were the same acts used with the 22-month-olds in Study 1.

After the model completed her actions, the child was observed for another 10 minutes of free play. An observer located behind a one-way mirror recorded the child's "distress" behavior, such as crying, fretting, attempts to leave the room, or remaining proximal to the mother, the child's speech, and how many of the modeled acts the infant imitated, if any. During the 10 minutes prior to and after the modeling, the mother and the model sat at opposite ends of the room and talked quietly.

Study 4

The data gathered in Study 1 indicated a major increase in performance on the cognitive tasks during the few months before the second birthday and relative independence of quality of performance on the various procedures. In order to evaluate the generality of these findings for a cross-sectional sample and to assess the effect of practice on the memory task, some of the procedures were administered to a sample of forty-nine children during one session which lasted a little over an hour. Twelve of these forty-nine children had participated in Study 2. The children, mainly Caucasian, middle class, and residing in the Cambridge area, belonged to one of four age groups: 19–20 months (n = 12), 22–23 months (n = 12), 25–26 months (n = 12), and 28–29 months (n = 13).

Four procedures were administered exactly as they had been to the two longitudinal cohorts in Study 1. These were memory for location, drawing a face, relational inference, and transposition. In addition, the mean length of utterance was computed from verbatim recordings of the child's spontaneous language obtained during a 20-minute play session. The single new procedure was a test of language comprehension. Children were asked the meaning of twenty-three words, using toys as props. As in Study 1, the child's responses were recorded by an observer in the adjacent room.

Study 5

The data gathered in the first four studies suggested that major changes in psychological functioning were occurring between 19 and 24 months of age. Although the nature of these changes was not clear as we planned a second longitudinal investigation, our thoughts centered on the hypothesis that during this period the child was coming to the realization that he could monitor and control his actions and evaluate his expectation of gaining self-generated goals. But we needed a richer corpus of observations in order to support or refute this tentative interpretation. Further, we wished to determine if the phenomena of Study 1 would be replicated in a home setting.

Six children, three boys and three girls, were selected, who were between 17 and 19½ months of age at the beginning of the observations. All the children were Caucasian, middle class and from the Cambridge area (see Table 2.2). The six were selected from a larger group of eighteen children of the same age. The final selection was based on the mother's motivation to remain cooperative for a 10-month period and the child's level of speech development. Children

Table 2.2. Demographic characteristics of six children (Study 5).

Subject	Sex	Ordinal position	Age when study began (mos.)	Mother's ed./occu.	Father's ed./occu.	Mother's age (yrs.)	Father's age (yrs.)
H	M	Only child	17	MD/pediatrician	MD/researcher	30	30
E	M	2nd-born (older sister)	17½	MA/counselor	3 yrs. college/builder	34	46
T	F	Only child	17¾	BA/nurse	MD/researcher	33	36
L	F	Only child	18½	BA/homemaker	BA/computer programmer	30	31
C	F	2nd-born (older sister)	19	PhD/professor	MD/physician	35	37
A	M	Only child	19½	MSW/homemaker	JD/lawyer	32	33

who either had just begun to speak or seemed about ready to speak their first meaningful words were chosen, in order to evaluate the concordance between the onset of speech and the performance on nonlinguistic tasks. Four of the children in the final sample were not yet speaking one-word utterances.

The basic set of observations came from thirteen to fourteen visits to the child's home, during which he or she was observed while playing with special sets of toys for approximately 40 minutes. The same two examiners visited the child's home every 3 weeks; one had worked on Study 1, the other was new to the staff. One of the examiners wrote down every language utterance and the context of that utterance, while the other examiner narrated into a tape-recorder a continuous description of the child's behavior with the toys and with each of the three adults. This corpus was used for two purposes. The language protocol was used to quantify both the mean length of utterance and the semantic and syntactic components of the child's language. The semantic analysis centered on references to standards, prohibitions, psychological states, and descriptions of the child's activity. The recorded behavioral narration was used to quantify changing patterns of interaction with the mother and the examiners as well as the changing quality of play.

A second source of data gathered during and after the period of free play was the child's reaction to specific experimental interventions. Some of these interventions were replications of procedures used in Study 1; others were new. In all cases one visitor acted as the examiner, while the second recorded the child's responses.

An initial visit to the home was made by one of the examiners one month before the official gathering of data, in order to acquaint the child and mother with the testing situation. During this initial session the child was allowed to play for about 20 minutes with a set of toys brought by the examiner. This period of play was followed by the first administration of the memory for location task.

The visits to the home, which occurred about every three weeks, consisted of nine procedures: symbolic play during which all spontaneous utterances by the child and the context of the utterances were recorded, imitation of and reaction to modeled acts, language comprehension, transposition, drawing a face, memory for location, imitation of sentences, oral commands, and stacking of blocks. As soon as the child was producing two-word utterances during her spontaneous play, two procedures were added: imitation of sentences and the ability to carry out oral commands.

The order of the administration of these procedures was standard for each child. However, the tempo of each session was determined, in part, by the child. Testing was conducted in a relaxed manner, allowing each child breaks for conversation, interaction with the mother, and food. If a child insisted on not performing a task, she was not pushed to do so. At the end of each task the examiners spoke with the mother. These conversations helped to maintain the mother's motivation and also provided some information about the child's behavior during the previous three weeks. The home visits varied in length from about 2 to 3 hours, depending upon the specific tasks administered and the child's cooperativeness.

Play session. The 40-minute symbolic play session, which was the first procedure to occur, was similar to the one used in Study 1. One of two similar sets of toys (57 toys in one set and 65 in the other) was used. The two sets were comprised of realistic representations of people, utensils, beds, food, and animals, as well as blocks. The toy sets were alternated so that each set was viewed every six weeks. During the play session the child's mother remained seated on a nearby couch or chair, along with one observer, who wrote down all of the child's language. This record consisted of a list of each of the child's utterances accompanied by a description of the context of the utterance. The second examiner was seated in a distant part of the room where she spoke quietly into a hand-held tape-recorder describing the play session. The mother was instructed not to encourage her child to play with any particular toy and only to interact if the child initiated it.

Reaction to modeling. After approximately 15 minutes of free play, usually when a natural break appeared in the child's play, the close observer and the mother joined the child on the floor in a quiet, unobtrusive manner. The observer then demonstrated a symbolic act with some of the toys already on the floor. She repeated the act slowly, making sure the child was watching, and then returned to her seat. The child was allowed to play with the toys for an additional 5 minutes. At the end of 20 minutes of play the observer again quietly joined the child and modeled a second, single act. After 25 minutes she modeled a third act. The single acts modeled on the fourteen visits were:

Visit	Single act
1	1. Examiner washes a black horse with a yellow cloth
	2. Small mother doll sleeps on a white block
	3. Ball with dots is made to eat a purple ring
2	1. Examiner sleeps on a pillow
	2. Blue block drinks an orange bottle
	3. Doll rides in an imaginary car

Visit	Single act
3	1. Doll is fed from a spoon
	2. Cloth jacket is put on a ball with dots in order to go outside
	3. Horse jumps over an imaginary fence
4	1. Wrench is used as a phone and put to examiner's ear
	2. Doll rides on an airplane
	3. Bolt is made to sit on a cup
5	1. Block, used as a car, is driven into a file box for a garage
	2. Juice is poured from a red measuring cup into a yellow round bolt
	3. Doll digs an imaginary hole with a shovel
6	1. Puppet eats a pear
	2. Bear rides in a cup
	3. Imaginary doll sleeps on a pillow in cradle
7	1. Doll pats a sheep
	2. Examiner washes a yellow cup in a container and wipes it dry with a cloth
	3. Blocks are sprinkled with an imaginary sprinkler
8	1. Monkey plays a drum, represented by teapot
	2. White ball, symbolizing a dog, eats from a yellow block
	3. Table is set with blocks, a screwdriver, and a real spoon
9	1. Cow looks through a blue ring, symbolizing a window
	2. Blue block, symbolizing a man, rides on a block, symbolizing a boat
	3. Doll falls, cries, and another doll, symbolizing mother, comes to nurture
10	1. Monkey hugs and rocks a smaller monkey
	2. Doll goes for a ride on a wrench, simulating a horse
	3. Crib symbolizes a shopping cart, while balls symbolize fruit and cereal
11	1. Ball is driven like a tractor
	2. Plane lands on a blue tub
	3. Baby horse is tired, and mother horse offers it a ride
12	1. Doll cares for a baby
	2. Doll washes dishes
	3. Doll spanks a child for eating cookies before dinner
13	1. A doll changes a baby's diapers
	2. A doll washes dishes in a blue sink
	3. A dog nips at a boy's pants and the boy taps him on the nose saying, "Don't bite."
	(Subject H only)
14	1. An animal sleeps on a cloth
	2. A doll wears a bracelet
	3. Cooking is simulated with a block and a stick

After about 30 to 35 minutes of play, the observer announced that she was going to play a new game, brought out a new set of toys, and again joined the mother and child on the floor. The child sat on the mother's lap, and the observer modeled a set of three acts in sequence, with the one exception that for one 27-month-old child only two acts were modeled. Each act was repeated slowly, making sure that the child watched the adult. The acts varied in difficulty according to the age of the child. The multiple acts that were modeled and their ages were:

Age (mos.)	Multiple acts
17–19	1. Doll talks on a small toy phone 2. Doll rides on a horse 3. Hat is put on a pig and pig walks outside
20–21	1. Bottle is fed to a toy zebra 2. Doll is put to bed 3. Doll's face is washed with a washcloth
22–26	1. Doll talks on a toy phone 2. Mother doll cooks a toy banana in a pan, and mother and father doll eat dinner with two plates 3. Three cows walk together, rain is simulated by hand motions, and the animals hide under a cloth
27 (Subject H only)	1. Two children, symbolized by blocks, talk to each other on a phone, also symbolized by a block 2. Wooden object, symbolizing a dog, falls in an imaginary mud puddle, is given a bath in a bucket, and is dried with a cloth

After the experimenter modeled the three acts in succession, as in Study 1 she invited the child to play and returned with the mother to the couch, leaving the child seated on the floor. Five minutes of additional play were recorded.

Language comprehension. After the play session and modeling, the toys were left on the floor, the tape-recorder was put away, the first observer again joined the child on the floor. If necessary, the child was allowed a recess to interact with the mother or have something to eat. The observer then administered a series of questions designed to assess the child's comprehension of language, while the other examiner wrote down the child's responses. The purpose of the procedure was to determine the child's comprehension of a previously prepared list of words. The words referred to parts of the body, food, household objects, animals, articles of clothing, vehicles, actions, qualities, and location. The nouns probed were: (parts of the body) *foot, head, hair, mouth, hand, teeth, finger, arms, lips, tongue, knee, elbow, thumb;* (food) *banana, orange, pear, apple;* (animals) *bear, cow, pig, giraffe;*

(household articles) *chair, table, door, window, floor, wall, lamp, couch, sofa, light, ceiling, pillow, plate, broom;* (clothing) *sock, shoe, shirt, pants;* and (other) *ball, airplane.* The transitive verbs were: *eat, throw, open, close, kiss, drink, blow, drop, hug, shake, step on, kick, push,* and *point to.* The intransitive verbs were: *sit, cry, jump, smile, run, crawl, stand, lie down, fall, turn around, dance,* and *fly.* And the adjectives and adverbs were: *soft, hard, moving, not moving, yellow, red, green, blue, littlest, biggest, smooth, rough, dirty, clean, bottom, top, up, down, full, empty, wet, dry, on, off, under,* and *over.*

The examiner began by asking the child about parts of the body and food, because these words are familiar to children this age. The examiner, using toys as props, asked questions in the form, "Can you show me your _____?" or, "Can you touch the _____?" or, "Where is the _____?" and waited for a response from the child. If the child did not respond, pointed to an incorrect object, or hesitated, the item was administered a second time later in the session.

Testing of the child's comprehension of verbs was accomplished by presenting the child with some object that could be used as an agent and asking the questions of the type, "Can you make the doll _____ the cow?" or asking the child to perform the action himself, "Can you _____ the cow?" Wherever possible, the child was asked to use objects in ways other than their usual stereotyped manner, such as "eating a cow." Testing continued until the child failed the easier items in each category or until the child became restless or bored and would no longer cooperate with the examiner.

Testing of verbs did not begin until the child responded correctly to some of the nouns. The assessment of knowledge of adjectives and adverbs was not administered until the child was successful on 75 percent of the nouns and verbs. Once an item passed reliably, it was not administered on subsequent visits. However, a few previously passed items were administered at the beginning of the procedure in order to engage the child's involvement.

Transposition. The near transposition problems for baby and daddy were administered as in Study 1.

Stacking blocks and copying a face. In the stacking blocks task, the first examiner placed two red plastic blocks in front of the child, stacked them vertically, and called the child's attention to the two-block tower. The examiner then handed the child a third block and asked, "Can you put another one on?" If the child successfully stacked the third block, the child was given additional blocks, one at a time, as long as the child was successful, or until a total of six blocks were stacked successfully. Testing was discontinued if the tower fell over several times, if the child refused to add blocks to the stack, or if the six-block tower was completed. The second examiner recorded the number of blocks stacked and noted the child's emotional behavior, such as clapping, refusal, or whining.

In the drawing task, the experimenter brought out a piece of white paper (2.25 x 2.80 dm) and a crayon and, while the child watched, drew a vertical line. The child was then asked to draw the line. If the child attempted to do so, the examiner then drew a circle on a separate piece of paper and invited the child to draw this form. When the child was able to draw a circle, the examiner drew a schematic face containing two eyes, a nose, and a mouth, and asked the child to draw the same face as described in Study 1. The line and circle tasks were administered at all of the sessions, even if the child had successfully drawn them on earlier home visits. Once the drawing of the face had been initiated with a particular child, it was administered on each subsequent visit.

Memory for location. Although the administration of this task was similar to that in Study 1, the apparatus was modified slightly to make it portable. Initially the child was familiarized with the task using one container and no screen. When the child had mastered that preliminary problem, the same container was used with the screen and a one-second delay. When the child found the reward, the test series began, and the procedure followed that in Study 1.

Sentence imitation. The purpose of this task was to assess the child's ability to repeat sentences of differing lengths and different meaning. The sentences belonged to one of three categories: action sentences, psychological state sentences, and obligation sentences. The items in the sentence imitation task were:

Action sentences
1. (Noun agent) sleeps
   _____ sleeps on bed
   _____ sleeps on big bed
2. _____ talks
   _____ talks on phone
   _____ talks on phone to daddy
3. _____ sits
   _____ sits on chair
   _____ sits on little chair

Psychological-state sentences
1. _____ wants
   _____ wants cup
   _____ wants more cups
2. _____ likes
   _____ likes cookies
   _____ likes more cookies

Obligation sentences

1. _____ has to
   _____ has to go
   _____ has to go to bed
2. _____ needs
   _____ needs hat
   _____ needs hat on head
3. _____ needs to wash
   _____ needs to wash hands
   _____ needs to wash dirty hands
4. _____ should eat
   _____ should eat apple
   _____ should eat big apple

The child sat near the examiner on the floor while she showed him an appropriate toy from among those on the floor. The examiner then asked the child, "Can you say (*the name of the object*)?" This word became the subject of the sentences that followed. If the child was able to repeat the single word, the examiner then asked the child to repeat a two-word sentence consisting of the object and a verb. If the child did this successfully, the examiner continued to add significant words to the sentence, asking the child to imitate each longer sentence.

The examiner discontinued this procedure when the child was unable to imitate the sentence after two consecutive trials or when the child imitated the entire sentence exactly. Action sentences were administered to all children first. When the child repeated a two-word action phrase, psychological state and obligation sentences were administered. The agents chosen as subjects for the sentences varied for each child, for they were words frequently used by that child.

One examiner administered the sentence imitation while the other wrote down the child's response. On each visit the child was first administered the single-word subject before the sentence was expanded. Once a sentence was repeated correctly, it was not administered again.

Oral commands. The purpose of this task was to assess the child's ability to remember and carry out commands differing in number of action units and content. The child sat on the floor near the examiner, who placed several toys appropriate to the task in front of the child. The examiner then asked the child to perform a two- or three-unit command. The two-unit commands to the child were:

1. Can you put the ball on the table and then give it to mommy?
2. Can you touch your nose and then clap your hands?
3. Can you make the doll go to sleep and then eat the banana?
4. Can you make the cow jump and then go into the box?

The three-unit commands were:

1. Can you drink from the cup, give me the spoon, and then touch your head?
2. Can you make the doll run, eat the apple, and ride the horse?

If the child completed an item successfully, it was not administered again. If the child failed an item, she was administered a second trial, but the testing of each command was discontinued after two consecutive failures. Three-unit commands were not administered until the child successfully completed a two-unit command. One examiner administered the task while the second wrote down the child's responses.

Study 6

In order to evaluate the generality of the major findings from Studies 1 and 5 on a non-Western sample of children, Katz (1981) gathered information on children growing up in the Fiji Islands. The sample included sixty-seven Fijian children between 13 and 36 months and thirty-one older children from 37 to 60 months of age. The children, primarily of Melanesian stock, lived in small villages of about a hundred people located on volcanic islands in the Fiji group. When there were no storms, which were frequent, the islands were accessible by a 10-hour boat journey from the capital. Each village was located on a bay between steep hillsides, near the mouth of a river or stream, and typically a 2-hour walk from the next village. A typical village consisted of houses, a church, one or two cooperative stores, and occasionally a community meeting house. A primary school adjoined every second or third village. The primary work in the villages was farming and fishing.

Each of the nine villages was visited about four times over the 13 months of data collection, and a total of sixty-seven children were tested more than once, with a period of several months between testings. The children were tested individually in their homes, either by a local assistant with Katz recording the children's responses or by Katz herself. Initially, the testing was done by the local assistant, but as Katz mastered the language and became familiar to the families, she took increasing responsibility for the testing. However, the age distribution of the children was equally broad throughout the early and later phases of the work. The battery included memory for location, linguistic inference, drawing a face, near transposition, and imitation of and reaction to modeled acts. The procedures were very similar to the ones used with the Western children, with some minor modifications.

Memory for location. In this procedure the receptacles that hid the prize (a piece of cracker) were drab-colored containers arranged in a circle rather than in a straight line and were covered with a cloth during the delay period. Additionally, the trials with identical containers were not administered to the Fiji children. Therefore, the maximum score was 12 (eight different receptacles with a 10-second delay).

Linguistic inference. Because manufactured toys were such novel stimuli for the Fijian children, ordinary household objects were used in this procedure (knife, small pot, piece of paper, cup, spoon). The meaningless objects were an odd-shaped plastic form, an oblong wooden form with a wooden tip, and a clear plastic nozzle. Additionally, the children were asked to give the requested object to the mother rather than to the examiner.

Drawing a face. The drawing task was administered exactly as described earlier.

Transposition. It was not possible in this task to use pieces of wood to represent the adult and infant because in Fijian one does not name inanimate objects with terms appropriate to living things. Thus seashells of different sizes were substituted for the wooden pieces. Otherwise the procedure was identical to the test of Cambridge subjects.

Reaction to modeling. In order to increase the naturalness of this procedure and accommodate to the expectations of the child and parent, the model interceded in the child's play after the child had been playing for 5 minutes rather than after 10 minutes. In addition, the child was given only eight toys with which to play, and two rather than three acts were modeled. The two acts were a doll eating and a doll going to sleep.

In the first act the model moved a spoon from a plate to the doll's mouth saying, "She is eating." For the act of sleeping, the examiner put a doll's head on a pillow and covered the doll with a cloth. For the children over 2 years of age who had been seen on a prior occasion, the eating sequence was elaborated a bit by having the examiner stir the spoon in a pot, spoon the food from the pot to the plate, and then feed the doll. After completing the acts, the examiner narrated the child's behavior into a tape-recorder. Distress was defined as the occurrence, within one minute of completion of the acts, of any one of the behaviors of crying, going to the mother's lap, inhibition of play, throwing of toys, or leaving the situation.

Study 7

The final study was a cross-sectional investigation intended to validate informal observations made in Studies 1 and 5. The observers noted that some children during the last half of the second year began to note accidental flaws in the integrity of toys, such as a crack in the plastic base of a telephone, a small tear in some clothing, a piece of dirt on a chair. The appearance of spontaneous concern with events that violated standards occurred at the same time that changes in other competences became obvious. But because the frequency of these actions was low, it was necessary to evaluate the validity of the informal observations.

A systematic comparison was made of ten 14-month-old and twenty-one 19-month-old children. The thirty-one subjects came individually with their mothers to the same play room used in Studies 1, 2, and 4. They were allowed to play for 20 minutes with a set of twenty-two toys. Ten toys were unflawed without irregularities or tears; these included a fire engine, a magnet, a car, a music box, a boat, an animal, and a wagon. However, another set of ten toys was purposely flawed in some way. Examples include a plastic boat with holes in the bottom, a doll with black streaks on the face, a doll with torn trousers, a broken telephone, an animal with the head missing, a white handkerchief with an irregular green streak, and a broken pencil. Additionally, two of the toys were odd-shaped, meaningless wooden pieces that were unflawed. The purpose of using these two toys was to test whether special concern with the flawed toys was due to the fact that the integrity of the toys was violated rather than to their discrepant quality. It was suspected that special attentiveness to the flawed objects would be due to the fact that their integrity had been violated and not because they were unusual.

An observer behind a one-way screen narrated the child's behavior into a recorder. After the 20-minute play session, this examiner joined the mother and child and presented to the child each of the flawed toys, one at a time, to see if the presentation provoked any special reaction. The examiner also asked the mother if she had noticed any concern with a violation of standards at home. The major variable of interest involved the behavior of the child during the 20-minute play session. The special reactions included pointing to the flaw in the toy and vocalizing about it, display of dysphoric affect while pointing to the toy, bringing only the flawed toys to the mother, or uttering any meaningful phrase which indicated that the child recognized that the toy was damaged, such as the comments, "It's broken," "Yuk," or "It's yukky."

Table 2.3. Major procedures administered in each of seven studies.

Sample	Spontaneous speech	Memory	Linguistic inference	Trans-position	Relational inference	Draw a face	Modeling	Symbolic play	Peer play	Language compre-hension	Oral commands	Sentence imita-tion	Stack blocks
Study 1 younger cohort	✓	✓	✓	✓	✓	✓	✓	✓	✓				
Study 1 older cohort	✓	✓	✓	✓	✓	✓	✓	✓	✓				
Study 2 cross-sectional group							✓						
Study 3 cross-sectional group							✓						
Study 4 cross-sectional group	✓	✓	✓	✓	✓	✓	✓			✓			
Study 5 longitudinal children	✓	✓		✓		✓	✓	✓		✓	✓	✓	✓
Study 6 Fiji children		✓	✓	✓		✓	✓						
Study 7 cross-sectional group								✓[a]					

a. Observers coded only the appreciation of flawed toys.

Reliability

The children's performances on the test procedures—namely memory, linguistic inference, transposition, relational inference, drawing, language comprehension, oral commands, sentence imitation, and stacking of blocks—were coded by one observer (see Table 2.3 for a summary of the procedures administered to each sample). The spontaneous speech protocols were scored for mean length of utterance on two different occasions with reliabilities ranging from .92 to .97. The symbolic and peer play data from Study 1 were coded from narrated recordings with reliabilities of .88 to .98. Finally, the children's reactions to the modeling were coded by two independent observers in Study 1 with reliabilities of .92 to .98. However, logistical considerations in Studies 5 and 6 made it impossible to have two independent observers code the child's distress reactions. In Study 5 one observer overheard the other narrating the child's behavior following modeling. In Study 6 it was not possible to enlist a Fijian informant to code reliably the infant's behavior with the American observer. This is one reason for the use of unambiguous behavioral signs of distress.

3

Signs of Self-Awareness

The entire corpus of data separated easily into a major and a minor theme. The more significant body of evidence suggests that, during the six months prior to the second birthday, children behave as if they are acquiring a new set of functions that centers on the sensitivity to standards and the ability to meet them, as well as an awareness of the self's behavioral effectiveness. The second theme concerns the growth of selected cognitive abilities during the second year of life and the relation between linguistic and nonlinguistic performances. Consider first the changes that announce the child's awareness of standards and ability to meet self-generated goals.

Appreciation of Standards

During the second half of the second year the children in Studies 1 and 5, for whom there was the richest set of relevant observations, and the older children in Study 7 began to display a concern with events and behaviors that violated states adults regard as normative. No 14-month-old in Study 7 behaved in any special way toward the flawed toys, while 57 percent of the 19-month-olds showed unambiguous signs of concern with one or more of these toys, (*chi* square = 5.8; $p < .05$). Some children pointed to one of the flawed toys and vocalized, others brought several of the toys to the mother, and a few children said explicitly that something about the toy was deviant ("Fix it," "Broke," "Yukky"). No child behaved this way toward the meaningless forms.

Although infants under one year are sensitive to events that deviate from the schemata they have created from experience (discrepant events), during the second year children react to events that appear to contrast with those which adults have indicated are proper. Children now point to small holes in clothing, tiny spots on furniture, a doll with chipped paint, a torn cord, missing bristles on a broom, a missing button on a dress, or an almost invisible crack in a plastic toy, and utter a negative, "Oh, Oh." Hundreds of events, many of them subtle and instrumentally irrelevant, capture the child's attention and, on occasion, elicit a reaction or verbal comment. Some one-word comments have the qualities of a conceptual category. One of the 22-month-old children in Study 5 consistently called a "boo-boo": any place where an upholstered button was missing on a chair or sofa, a bowel movement, dirt on the floor, and a broken toy telephone. These events share no common physical quality. What they do share is that each is a variation on a normative experience which presumably has been associated with a communication or action from parents indicating that the event is disapproved. Subject L at 27 months held a doll over a toy toilet and said, "Now pee." A few seconds later she said, "Her nose is running." The close temporal contiguity between the two statements suggests that the first may have evoked the second. The dimension they share is that both actions are undesirable from the parents' point of view and both are probably being socialized.

Bloom (1973) noted that her daughter Alison used the word *dirty* to refer to an empty bag, a diaper, and a doll being shaken in a cup in a sequence simulating the bathing of the doll. Bühler (1935) also noted an increase in sensitivity to parental standards during the second year. She described an experiment in which 1- and 2-year-old children were forbidden to touch a toy by an adult. When the adult left the room briefly, many of the infants touched the toy. But when the adult returned, "60 percent of the 1;4 and 100 percent of the 1;6 show the greatest embarrassment, blush, and turn to the adult with a frightened expression. From 1;9 on they attempt to make good what has happened by returning the toy quickly to its place" (p. 67).

In an essay concerned with adult speech to young children (baby-talk) across six languages (Arabic, Marathi, Comanche, Gilyak, English, and Spanish), Ferguson (1964) noted that among the most frequent words were references to evaluative qualities (good and bad). The word *kix*, meaning "dirty, don't touch," occurs in almost every language of the Middle East.

The language protocols from the children in Study 5 revealed that the age when their speech first referred to standards (*broken, boo-boo, dirty, wash hands, can't, hard do*) ranged from 19 to 26 months. All children produced this class of utterance. Similar data gathered by others indicate that by 20 months most children are using words that refer to standards (*bad, good, hard, dirty, nice*). The sources of this information are both English and German and include a 1928 diary by Stern and Stern. The remarkable agreement in the time when children first use evaluative language implies the maturation of a new cognitive function (Bretherton, McNew, and Beeghly-Smith, 1981).

Distress to Modeling

Perhaps the most significant observation was the appearance of signs of anxiety or distress after the examiner modeled the acts in front of the child. Distress was defined as the occurrence of any one of the following behaviors during the minute after the model completed her actions: fretting, crying, clinging to the mother, absence of any play with toys during the minute, and protestations indicating the child did not want to play or wanted to leave the room. The most frequent distress reactions were nonverbal and included clinging to the mother, inhibition of play for the entire minute, and fretting or crying. The behavioral signs of distress appeared first at around 15 months, grew quickly with age, and reached a peak just before the second birthday (see Fig. 3.1; Table 3.1). One child in Study 1 said, while clinging to the mother, "It's Mommy's turn to play." Another child who did not manipulate the toys eventually gave one of the relevant toys to the

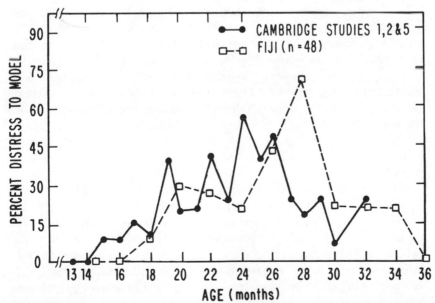

Fig. 3.1. Percentage of Cambridge and Fijian children showing distress to the model.

Table 3.1. Percentage of children showing distress to the model (Study 1).

	Younger cohort			Older cohort	
Age (mos.)	Realistic toys	Nonrealistic toys	Age (mos.)	Realistic toys	Nonrealistic toys
13	0	29	20	6	0
14	0	29	21	13	6
15	7	21	22	31	38
16	7	43	23	25	63
17	14	29	24	56	50
18	14	29	25	44	38
19	29	43	26	44	31
20	7	43	27	27[a]	
21	21	21	28	20	
22	14	36	29	27	
			30	7	
			32	27	

a. From 27 to 32 months there was one session of modeling in which both realistic and nonrealistic toys were used.

mother and said, "Do it." When the mother indicated that the child should play, the boy went to the corner of the room and began to sob. Another girl fretted, insisted she wanted to go home, and then threw some toys against the door.

In Study 1 distress following modeling with the realistic toys showed a curvilinear function, with maximal distress at 24 months when 56 percent of the older children showed some behavioral signs of distress (the statistical test for a quadratic trend was significant at $p < .01$). No 13- or 14-month-old showed distress to the model with the realistic toys, and only 27 percent of the 29-month-olds showed distress following modeling. When the modeling was performed with the nonrealistic toys, the function was similar for the older children. No 20-month-old child in Study 1 showed distress, 63 percent showed distress at 23 months, and the occurrence of distress declined to 31 percent at 26 months.

However, more younger children in Study 1 showed signs of distress to the unrealistic than to the realistic toys because they were probably not cognitively mature enough to become actively involved with the unrealistic toys for a long period of time. Hence they became bored before the 10 minutes of play were completed and prior to the model's intervention. At every age from 13 to 22 months the proportion of younger children showing distress during the 10 minutes prior to the model's intervention was greater than the proportion showing distress during the one minute after the model's actions. This pattern did not occur with the realistic toys. Further, the older children did not show irritability with either the unrealistic or realistic toys prior to the model's actions. Thus the occurrence of distress among the younger cohort following modeling with the unrealistic toys cannot be interpreted as evidence of a specific reaction to her behavior but may be continuation of the distress created by boredom generated during the previous 10 minutes.

When the criterion of distress was restricted to the single, least ambiguous variable of crying within one minute following the model's actions with the unrealistic toys, the data of Study 1 revealed a sharp increase in distress from 0 percent at 20 months for both the younger and older children to 31 percent at 23, 24, and 25 months. By 29 months, however, no child cried after the model's action.

The distress does not seem to be due to the number of prior exposures to the model. At 23 months, when the children in the older cohort had been exposed to the model on six prior occasions, five showed signs of distress with the realistic toys. When the younger cohort was 16 months old, they, too, had visited the laboratory on six prior occasions, but only one child showed any distress. Despite the fact that the younger and older cohorts had markedly different numbers of visits to the laboratory, when each group was 20 months old, the proportion of children showing distress was similar. Further, among the 22- to 23-month-old children in Study 2, who had only one experience with the model, 50 percent showed distress following the model's action. Because this proportion is greater than the 31 percent in the older cohort, it is possible that the familiarity of the examiner is a factor affecting the probability of distress. But clearly the age of the child is more critical for the distress reaction than the number of prior visits.

In Study 5 the examiner modeled acts on four separate occasions during each visit to the home. On the first three occasions, a novel single act was displayed; that is, the single acts were different on each visit to the home. On the fourth occasion, which occurred at the end of the play session, the examiner modeled three acts in succession. The modeling of three acts presumably generated greater uncertainty in the child because of the greater difficulty in assimilating and recalling the model's behavior.

A number of children showed behavioral signs of distress after single and multiple acts within one minute after the model had completed her actions when the criteria for distress were the same ones used in Study 1 (see Table 3.2). As with the children in Study 1, distress was infrequent prior to 19 months and most frequent from 19 to 23 months. The first appearance of distress occurred at 17

Table 3.2. Number of children displaying distress following modeling of single and multiple acts by age (Study 5).

Ages (mos.)	Single act	Multiple acts	Single or multiple acts
17–18	1	0	1
18–19	0	0	0
19–20	3	2	4
20–21	2	3	4
21–22	2	2	2
22–23	3	3	5
23–24	1	2	2
24–25	1	2	3
25–26	2	1	2
26–27	1	3	4

months for one child, 19 months for three children, 20 months for one, and 22 months for one child. All six children showed distress on at least one occasion by 22 months of age; most did so on several occasions. Distress occurred in all children prior to the appearance of any speech that referred to standards for the child's performance or feelings of incompetence. These linguistic expressions occurred after 23 months. Unlike the laboratory room in Study 1, the home setting was familiar, and the two women became increasingly familiar to and friendly with the child on each succeeding visit to the home. Nonetheless, the first appearance of distress for five of the children occurred after several visits to the home, not on the initial visits. The distress does not seem to be a reaction to the unfamiliarity of the setting or the examiner.

In Study 3, which was performed in the Wake Forest laboratory, behavioral signs of distress occurred in 83 percent of the 24-month-olds and 63 percent of the 18-month-olds. The higher frequency of distress, compared with the data from Study 1, is most likely due to the fact that simply remaining "proximal to the mother" was coded as an index of distress. Though a common behavior, this was not used as an index of distress in Studies 1, 5, and 6; in Study 1 distress was coded only if the child clung to the mother.

Few Fiji children in Study 6 displayed distress prior to 20 months, even though many showed fearfulness toward the doll, which was a novel object for these children. There was no correlation between distress to the model and to the doll. There was a steep rise to a peak distress of 72 percent at 27 months, followed by a sharp decline. There was only a 3-month difference between the age of peak distress to modeling with realistic toys in the Fijian children and Cambridge samples in Studies 1, 2, and 5 (Fig. 3.1).

Finally, as part of her unpublished doctoral dissertation, Gellerman followed a longitudinal sample of five Vietnamese children who had recently arrived with their parents in the United States. None of the families spoke English well, and all were just becoming acclimated to their new society. The children were seen at home every two to three weeks, beginning at 15 to 17 months of age through 26 to 28 months. The modeling procedure was similar to that used in Study 5. None of the children showed distress to the modeled acts during the initial visits to the home, but all displayed obvious signs of distress between 17 and 24 months.

This developmental function may reflect the emergence of several related processes. First, the child may experience an obligation to implement the acts of the model together with an awareness of her inability to implement the action, either because the child forgot what the model did or because the child is unsure of her ability to do so. As a result, the child becomes uncertain and may begin to cry or stop playing. The possibility of complete memory failure can be eliminated, for in many cases, seven or eight minutes after the distress reaction when the child had left the mother's side and begun to play again, she would display an exact or fragmented version of one of the model's prior actions. There may have been a temporary forgetting of the model's behavior, but it was not permanent.

The distress to the model implies that the child has some awareness of his ability, or lack of ability, to meet the standard represented by the model's action. But faith in this interpretation requires elimination of the possibility that the distress was due simply to the adult's interruption of the child's play. Studies 2 and 3, which were implemented to control for that possibility, revealed that distress was infrequent when the examiner simply interrupted the child's play. Only three of nineteen children in Study 2 showed any distress under this condition. By contrast, one half of the children showed distress within one minute after seeing the woman model the three acts. Six children in this group cried, one turned away from the woman and said, "Don't watch me," and two children clung tightly to their mothers. None of these nine children showed any of these behaviors during the 10 minutes prior to the modeling; all had played happily during the 10 minutes prior to the model's intervention. A comparison between Groups 1 and 2 of Study 2 for distress versus no distress yielded a chi-square of 3.35 (1 df, $p < .05$, one tail). In Study 3 only 8 percent of the children showed distress on the day when the model simply interrupted their play, as compared to 73 percent when the model displayed a coherent action. Thus it seems fair to conclude that the signs of distress are not produced by the adult simply interrupting the child's play. The act of modeling some coherent action is critical for the affective phenomenon.

The occurrence of distress in Study 3 was correlated with a failure to imitate the model. Each child was assigned a distress score based on the combined occurrence of crying and attempts to leave the room for the 5 minutes prior to modeling and the first 5 minutes after modeling, the maximum score being 15. Among the infants who imitated at least one modeled act, 43 percent showed a lower distress score after modeling than before, and 19 percent had a higher score. Among those who failed to imitate, 41 percent showed a higher distress score after modeling and 23 percent had a lower score.

An age by occurrence of imitation analysis of variance performed on the distress scores for the first 5 minutes of post-modeling revealed a significant effect for imitation (F, $[1, 44] = 6.36$, $p < .05$). An age by imitation analysis of variance performed on the infant's distress scores during the last 5 minutes of pre-modeling revealed nonsignificant main effects and a nonsignificant interaction. A comparable analysis for the session when the toys were simply scattered, with the imitation score recorded on the modeling day serving to classify the infant as an imitator or nonimitator, revealed no influence of age, imitation, or an age by imitation interaction.

Because slightly fewer children in Study 2 were distressed when the mother, rather than the less familiar examiner, was the model (two out of twelve compared to nine out of eighteen), the familiarity of the social relationship between child and adult may monitor the likelihood or intensity of the state of uncertainty. The average 2-year-old has seen the mother display "actions" on many occasions; some may have been contexts in which the mother was attempting to persuade the child to imitate her. It is likely that the child did not always imitate the mother on all of these occasions, and the child had many opportunities to extinguish the feeling of obligation to imitate the mother every time she displayed a coherent action. Additionally, because the child had a less familiar relationship with the model, it is possible that she felt a stronger press to display the acts modeled by the less familiar person. The uncertainty in the social relationship may motivate the child to be concerned with the model's possible reactions to her. As a result, the child is vulnerable to increased apprehension when the acts are modeled because of a self-imposed obligation to perform actions that she is not sure she can implement. If the child felt no obligation to imitate the model, she would not pass to the second stage of uncertainty over duplicating the acts witnessed. These data reveal the exquisitely sensitive dependence of behavior on subtle dimensions in the social context.

Mastery Smiles

The distress that followed the modeling implies that the child has some awareness of what is competent performance. In order to determine if this awareness would be revealed spontaneously, the occurrence of smiling in association with task mastery was coded in Study 5. This decision was based on the common observation that children and adults occasionally smile following their completion of a task or their comprehension of an initially complex idea.

The observer noted every occasion of smiling and the associated context during each of the 40-minute symbolic play sessions in Study 5. The smiles were classified by the two observers after listening to the recorded narration of the session as belonging to one of six categories. The two observers discussed the narration until they agreed on the category. If they could not agree, the smile was coded as ambiguous.

The first category was social smiles. The child looked at one of the adults and smiled either spontaneously or as a reaction to the adult's behavior or facial expression. The child was not engaging in any activity, and the smile appeared to be a form of greeting or acknowledgment of the adult.

The second category was discrepancy smiles. The child smiled to an unexpected, discrepant event in the environment or one that was not purposely produced by the child (for example, the wind knocked down an object; the child accidentally hit a toy that made a noise).

The third class referred to smiles accompanying games. The child smiled as an accompaniment to gamelike interactions between himself and one or more of the adults, or he smiled in anticipation of a gamelike interaction.

Fourth were smiles on hearing one's name. The child smiled when he heard one of the adults talk about him or mention his name, which was infrequent.

The fifth category, mastery smiles, referred to smiles that accompanied the child's solitary activity with objects, the labeling or categorization of objects, the production of a discrepancy purposefully, as when the child made an odd noise with his mouth and then smiled. It also included the testing of limits, as when the child touched a vase he was not supposed to touch; and smiles that occurred after an adult conformed to the child's request or direction. In all of these contexts the child either was engaged in or had completed a goal-directed activity.

The final category was ambiguous smiles. This referred to smiles for which it was not possible to agree on the immediate incentive for the response.

The three most frequently occurring categories were social smiles, mastery smiles, and ambiguous smiles. The growth functions for the social and mastery smiles were plotted for each of the six children (see Fig. 3.2). The growth functions for T and L were different from those of the other four children. Social smiles were more frequent than mastery smiles on the initial visits, but after 20 months mastery smiles gained in frequency. For the other four children the growth functions for the two classes of smiles were similar but the difference between mastery and social smiles was significantly larger after 19 months than before ($t = 5.00$ df 5, $p < .01$). For five of the children, the difference between social and mastery smiles was largest between 20 and 24 months; this is the time when distress to the model was also maximal for most children.

Mastery smiles may be interpreted as signifying that the child generated a goal for an external action sequence, persisted in his attempts to gain that goal, and smiled upon attainment. As many investigators

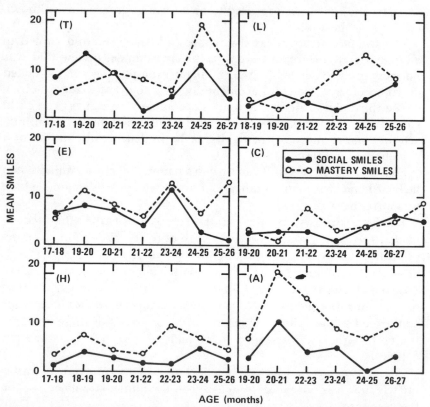

Fig. 3.2. Growth functions for social and mastery smiles for six longitudinal children.

have noted, one occasion for the smile is the assimilation of an external event to a schema, as when a 4-month-old smiles to the presentation of a human face. In the case of mastery smiles, the response is released when the child perceives he has attained the cognitive representation of a previously generated goal after investment of effort. This assumption awards to the older child not only a disposition to generate goals, but also the competence to know when that goal has been reached. It is important to note that mastery smiles were independent of indexes of language development.

Many observers have noted that children under 16 months will smile as an accompaniment to their action—one-year-olds smile after standing up or knocking a dish off their highchair. But one-year-olds are less likely to select a goal to be reached through their own actions, persist over a period of minutes in a continuous attempt to attain the goal, and then smile upon attaining it. There is an important difference between the smile that accompanies the use of simple motor coordinations, such as jumping, walking, or hitting an object, and the smile that follows prolonged investment of goal-directed effort which serves a previously generated plan. The smile that follows this latter class of behavior appears after the first birthday and shows a major enhancement during the last half of the second year.

Directives to Adults

The ability to generate goals was also revealed in the children's social interactions with the mother and the two observers. Reflection on the behavior of the children in Study 5 led to the creation of a small set of variables, which were first coded from the narrated recordings made by the two observers. Later the main author, who had not participated in the original coding, listened to a random sample of one-third of these recordings and independently scored the same variables coded earlier by the observers. The reliabilities between the author and the observers for individual variables for the six children were between 95 and 98 percent.

One of the variables, called directives to adults, refers to three subclasses of similar responses, directed usually to the mother but occasionally to one of the two observers. In all three subclasses the child attempted to alter the behavior of the adult. The least frequent subclass was a request for a specific object (food, pillow, or toy). In order for this category to be coded, the child had to indicate, unambiguously, that she wanted the object. Intelligible speech was not necessary. During the early months of the study the child might whine and utter her special vocalization for *pillow* or *cookie*. Or she would merely point to the cookie, look at her mother, and fret. When speech became intelligible, coding of this response was easy. This class of responses, which made up less than 10 percent of all the responses coded as "directives to adults" first occurred in some children late in the first year or early in the second year (e.g., the child of 14 months pulled her mother to the door or pointed to a toy she wanted).

The other two subclasses involve either changing the behavior of an adult or requesting help with a problem the child was working on but could not solve. The two behaviors, which were equally frequent, did not ordinarily occur until the middle of the second year. Common examples of the former included putting a toy telephone to the mother's ear and gesturing or vocalizing in a way to indicate that the child wanted the mother to talk on the telephone, pointing to a place in the room to indicate that the child wanted the mother to sit there or move to that location, or giving the mother a doll and a toy bottle and indicating that he wanted the mother to feed the doll.

In this category the child indicated by gesture or gesture and vocalization that he wanted the adult to behave in a specific manner. The goal seemed to be to produce a specific behavior in the adult. Unlike similar behaviors in one-year-olds, the child wanted no material object. Often the child had the mother move in one direction and then several minutes later, indicated that he wanted her to move back to her original location. Requests for the mother to engage in game-like interactions, which a mother would not ordinarily implement because they were childlike, appeared late in the observations. For example, the child asked the mother to talk on the toy telephone, make funny noises, drink from an empty cup, or repeat an action the child had just displayed. This response can be interpreted as reflecting the fact that the child realizes certain behavior is characteristic of children and that, therefore, to request a mother to perform such an action is a violation of a normative standard. It can be argued that the child is able to make such requests only when he has some conception of the differences between appropriate actions for the child and adult roles.

The third subclass involves requests for instrumental aid with a problem. The child, for example, would be working at a puzzle, experience difficulty, and go to the mother indicating she wanted assistance. Typically, these occurrences involved help with a puzzle, wanting the mother to open or close a box, or wanting the mother to put a dress on a doll after she had tried to do so unsuccessfully. Additionally, the child might want the mother to help her get up on a chair or down from a sofa.

Common to all three subclasses—requests for objects, requests for the adult to behave in a particular manner, and requests for help with a problem—is the directing of an adult to behave in a specific way. This category is illustrated in the behavior of four of the subjects —T, H, C, and E—whose ages are given to the nearest quarter month:

SUBJECT T

Age (mos.)   *Examples*

17¾   T hands the mother a phone and says, "Do, do." (This is a game the mother and child plays in which the mother talks on the telephone.)

18½   T makes motions to the mother indicating she wants to be picked up. T hands the mother a telephone, the mother gives it back to her, but T says, "No, no," and pushes the phone to the mother.

21¼   After T does a modeled act, she puts the toys on her mother's lap and says, "Ma, ma, ma, ma."

22   T wants a phonograph record put on the phonograph and says, "En keet."

23   T hands a doll and bottle to her mother, indicating she wants her mother to feed the doll. T requests her mother to take her feet off the sofa and put them on the floor, saying, "En ya shoe."

24¾   T indicates by gesture she wants her mother to open a box, close the box, put a bib on a doll, and dress a doll.

SUBJECT H

17   H brings a puzzle to the mother and indicates by gesture he wants her to place a piece in the puzzle.

19¾   H pulls on the mother because he wants a cracker in the kitchen.

22¾   H asks for his pillow, saying "pill."

24   H wants help in opening a box and with a puzzle.

27   H puts a phone to the examiner's ear, wanting her to speak. H wants the examiner to drink some tea.

SUBJECT C

20½   C wants help in putting a blanket on a doll.

21   C wants the examiner to move to the other side of the couch, and points to the place where she wants the examiner to sit.

21¾   C wants the mother to talk on the phone. C wants the mother to take off the doll's dress after she has invested some effort in trying to do so.

22   C wants her mother to move over on the couch.

SUBJECT E

17½   E requests some food, directs his mother to sit in a particular place, and asks for help in opening a box.

SUBJECT E

Age (mos.) *Examples*

19   E asks for toys and for help in opening a box, getting up on mother's lap, and doing a puzzle. E wants his mother to make a crying noise like a young child.

19¾   E wants one of the examiners and the mother to hug a toy bear, as he had done earlier.

21   E wants the examiner to bite one of the toy animals. E asks one of the examiners to say "ruff," as he had done earlier. E wants the examiner to pretend to eat a toy banana, as he had done. E wants the examiner to allow him to feed her from a toy bottle.

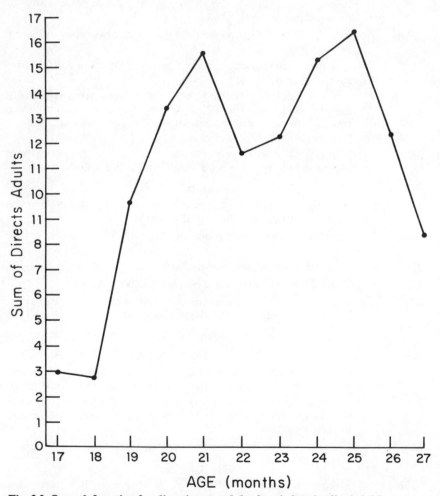

Fig. 3.3. Growth function for directives to adults for six longitudinal children.

The growth function for all three subclasses of the directives to adults category was not altered when consideration was given only to requests for help with a problem and requests that the adult conform to the child's directions. Thus, the pooling of all three subclasses of behavior probably did not distort the growth function for this variable.

All six children in Study 5 displayed an increase in directives to adults over the first ten to twelve home visits; 90 percent of these acts were directed at the mother (see Figs. 3.3–3.9). The function was low at 17 and 18 months and reached a peak value for each of the children between 20 to 25 months. The function was steepest between 18 and 21 months for E, A, L, and C and steepest between 22 and 24 months for H and T, and it underwent a slight decline at 26 and 27 months (the quadratic trend was not significant).

The four children in Study 5 who showed the first peak early, at 21 to 22 months, in later sessions asked the mother to behave in a childlike manner or requested permission to initiate acts that were normally prohibited by the mother. The decline after the first peak

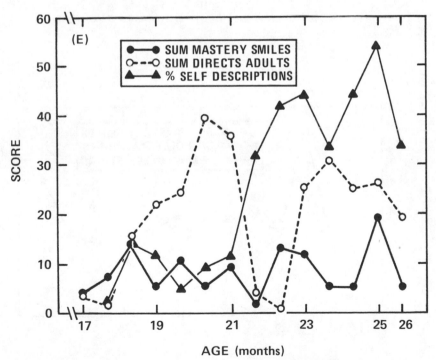

Fig. 3.4. Growth functions for mastery smiles, directives and self-descriptions for E.

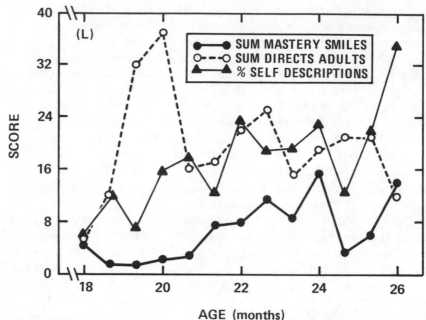

Fig. 3.5. Growth functions for mastery smiles, directives and self-descriptions for L.

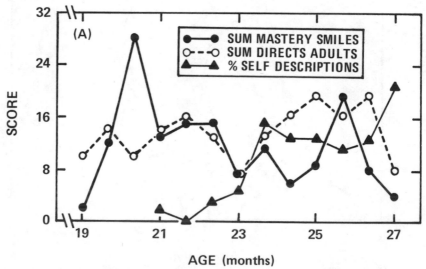

Fig. 3.6. Growth functions for mastery smiles, directives and self-descriptions for A.

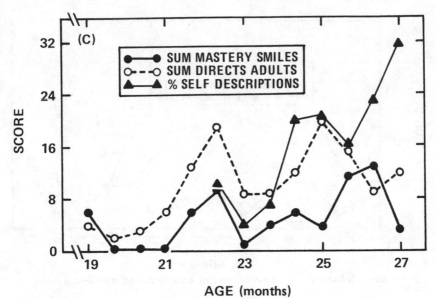

Fig. 3.7. Growth functions for mastery smiles, directives and self-descriptions for C.

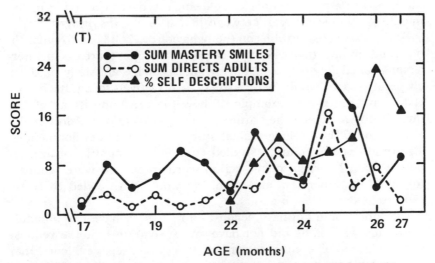

Fig. 3.8. Growth functions for mastery smiles, directives and self-descriptions for T.

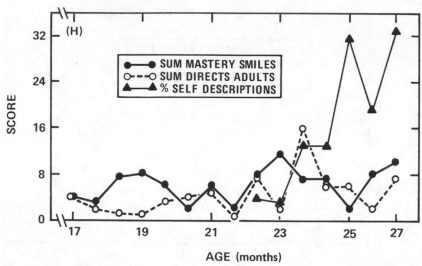

Fig. 3.9. Growth functions for mastery smiles, directives and self-descriptions for H.

corresponded to the time when the child showed distress to the model. Thus, it is likely that the inhibition of spontaneity that typically followed distress to the model's acts resulted in fewer attempts to direct or command the mother or the observers. Gellerman's longitudinal study of five Vietnamese children also showed a growth function for directives to adults that paralleled the one found in Study 5 with a peak number of relevant responses occurring in the middle set of observations, between 18 and 24 months of age.

Hay's (1979) observations on the behavior of 12-, 18-, and 24-month-old children and their mothers revealed a major increase in interactions called "cooperative" during the second year. Many of these cooperative acts would be classified as directives to adults in our coding system, a nice example of how the presuppositions of the investigator influence the nature of his classifications. Additionally Benedict (1979), in a longitudinal study of language development in eight middle-class children studied from 9 to 27 months of age, reported that 32 percent of the action words produced were requests for an adult to perform an action. We would have coded these responses as directives to adults.

The child would not have begun to direct the behavior of an adult in specific ways if he did not have an expectation that the request would be met. The enhancement of this response is evidence that the child expects he can influence the behavior of others. It is true that 8-month-olds also point to desired objects and whine, as if indicating they want the object and are attempting to direct the adult's behavior. But, we suggest, at this earlier age infants have no conscious conception that the cry or gesture will change the behavior of the adult. The response simply follows their seeing the desired object or their frustration at not having it. The pointing or whining of the 8-month-old infant superficially resembles the request for help with a puzzle seen in a 20-month-old. But as nineteenth century observers argued, the two responses are profoundly different with respect to the underlying cognitive competences. The monkey, the 4-month-old baby, and the 2-year-old child all can be operantly conditioned to make a motor response when it is followed by a reinforcement consisting of a change in visual stimulation. But this similarity does not mean that the accompanying cognitive processes are necessarily the same in all three organisms—even though Griffin (1976) argued that because animal communication shares properties with human language, it is reasonable to suggest that animals "have mental experiences and communicate with conscious intent" (p. 104).

The request of the 20-month-old seems to differ from that of the younger child in at least two ways. First, the older child recognizes that the adult's reaction is necessary to gain the goal; indeed in some cases it is the goal. Second, the older child has an expectation that the adult will respond appropriately. But it will require additional observations of a subtle sort to verify these claims.

Self-Descriptive Utterances

The speech of the six children in Study 5 provided additional evidence for the growth of functions seemingly related to the awareness of the self's behavior. All the utterances and their contexts during the 40-minute play session were recorded by one of the observers. Ambiguities were resolved by listening to the taped record of the play session. Over 90 percent of the utterances were spontaneous remarks rather than replies to the mother's questions or parts of conversations. We concentrated on the children's spontaneous utterances, rather than purposely engaging them in conversation, because of an interest in spontaneous changes in semantic reference. Dialogue constrains the child.

As others have reported, when speech first emerges, the vast majority of one-word utterances name objects in the child's visual field. The child looks at, touches, points, or picks up a toy and says its name. The next most frequent class of utterance during the first stage of speech is to communicate a desire for an object or event, noted by the word *more*, or by pointing to an object and saying its name with the high-pitched tone of voice that signifies a frustrated need. The distinctive timbre of this utterance is easily differentiated from one that simply names an object.

The study was not primarily concerned with the growth of syntax during this first period of language development, an issue that has already been addressed by Brown (1973), Bloom (1973), Bowerman (1973), Clark (1973), Greenfield and Smith (1976), Schesinger (1971; 1974), and Slobin (1977), but mean length of utterance (MLU) was scored using Brown's recommended procedure. MLU was computed only when a child provided at least 50 intelligible utterances on a particular visit. Typically, MLU for each session was based on between 100 and 150 spontaneous utterances.

MLU rose steadily with age for each child (see Fig. 3.10). The two children—a boy and a girl—who spoke earliest had the highest MLU values (over 4.0) at the end of the period of observation. Three children (one boy and two girls) began to speak a few months later. Two of these three children completed the study with MLU values between

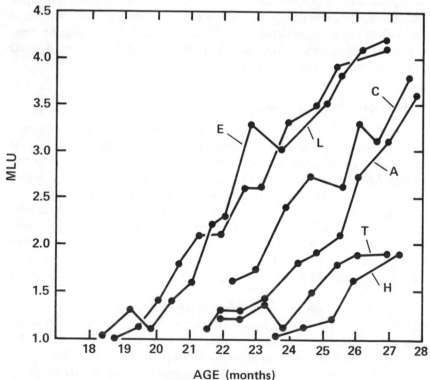

Fig. 3.10. Growth of MLU for six longitudinal children.

3.5 and 4.0, while the third had an MLU of less than 2.0 at 27 months when the study ended. The boy who was the last to begin to speak had an MLU of 1.9 at the end of the study. Thus, there was great variability in MLU among the six children in Study 5, despite the fact that all were from middle- or upper-middle-class families. The range of MLU at 27 months was from 1.9 to 4.2.

All utterances that were either immediate repetitions of a word or phrase just uttered by an adult or replies to adult questions were not scored; these comprised less than 1 percent of all the child's utterances. Three major semantic variables were coded: utterances that refer to objects or qualities of objects ("horse," "leg," "big horse," "horsey hurt"), utterances that describe either the appearance or the action of one of the adults in the room ("mommy sit"), and utterances that describe the child's actions, called "self-descriptive utterances."

Self-descriptive utterances were defined narrowly to include only utterances that occurred when the child was engaged in an action and spoke a word or sentence referring to that action ("climb'" as the child was climbing up on a chair, or "up" as the child tried to get up on a box) and utterances containing the words *I, my, mine,* or the child's name, together with a predicate ("My book," "I sit," "Tina eat"). If the utterance referred only to an object (the child said "doll" as he was playing with a doll), it was not scored as a self-descriptive utterance.

Once the child began to speak two- and three-word utterances, there was little difficulty in deciding whether a phrase was self-descriptive. The ambiguity only arose with single-word utterances. But all decisions were conservative; if there was any doubt, the utterance was not scored as self-descriptive. The average reliability coefficient for the coding of these three variables was .95, with a range of .91 to .98.

Self-descriptive utterances were absent during the early visits, and their most common form when they first appeared was a single word referring to an action or location while the child was engaged in a relevant behavior. The child might say "up" as he climbed up on a sofa, or "go" as he went to a door. By 22 months, when the pronoun *I* or the child's name appeared, the most common usage was *I* plus an action predicate ("I go," "I do," "I play"). By 23 to 24 months, a frequent class of self-descriptive utterances included the predicates *can, can't,* and *want.* By the final visits, at 26 and 27 months, self-descriptive utterances were sophisticated, including phrases like, "I step on my ankle" or "I do it myself." All six children showed similar growth functions for this variable, with most showing a major increase in self-descriptive utterances between 19 and 24 months (See Figs. 3.4–3.9). Some children displayed an asymptote early, some later.

Four of the six children showed similar proportions of self-descriptive utterances (about a third of all utterances at 27 months).

Bloom, Lightbown, and Hood (1975) collected a similar set of language protocols from four children over the course of repeated visits to the children's homes. Two children were observed from 19 to 25 months, one child from 21 to 24 months, and one child from 21 to 25 months. Although the coding categories used were different from those in Study 5, including categories of action, location, intention, state, their report contained a representative sample of about 200 to 290 utterances for each child over the period of observation. When these data were coded for self-descriptive utterances, the proportion of such utterances was remarkably similar for the four children (34 to 35 percent). This value is comparable to the proportion of self-descriptive utterances shown in Study 5 by Subject E at 25 months and to the values for the four other subjects at 27 months. Thus, despite differences in the context of observation and intention of the investigator, both studies reveal that about one third of a 2-year-old's utterances are descriptive of the self's actions.

Bloom (1973) also recorded the speech of her daughter during the second year of life and noted that from 17 to 20 months the child began to use five verb forms frequently: *tumble, back, tire, catch,* and *turn.* The contexts in which these forms appeared suggested that they accompanied the child's actions and therefore fit the category of self-descriptive utterances.

Rodgon, Jankowski, and Alenskas (1977) provided supportive data on three children studied during the second year of life. The investigators explicitly noted the action context that accompanied the children's single-word utterances. The children most often spoke when they were performing an action. But more significant, 33 to 51 percent of the utterances for all three children occurred when they were performing an action with a relevant object, in short, a self-descriptive utterance. By contrast, only 1 to 6 percent of the utterances described the actions of another person with a relevant object; these data are remarkably comparable to those in Study 5. These investigators commented on the relatively sudden increase in the self-descriptive utterances of one boy who was observed from 16 to 20 months: "Linguistic relations involving action are not expressed by Brian at the very beginning of single-word usage, but appear rather suddenly at a point still early in language acquisition" (p. 41).

Examination of the MLU values for different proportions of self-descriptive utterances in Study 5 revealed that the frequency of self-descriptive utterances was independent of the child's MLU, for the range of MLU values for differing proportions of self-descriptive utterances was large. For Subject H, 20 percent of his utterances were self-descriptive with an MLU of 1.2, while Subject A had the same proportion of self-descriptive utterances with an MLU of 3.6. When the proportion of self-descriptive utterances was 30 percent or more, Subject L had an MLU of 3.1 and Subject H had an MLU of 1.2.

L, who spoke early, uttered self-descriptive utterances early. But once H began to speak, which he did not do until after two years of age, the proportion of his utterances that were descriptive of self for the period 25 to 27 months was similar to that of L, despite large differences in MLU between the two children.

The increase in self-descriptions was due not simply to the increased frequency of verbs and modifiers, and was accompanied by a decrease in the proportion of utterances that named or described objects and their qualities. For five of the six children there was a decline, with age, in utterances that described objects, and the age when there was a sharp decline in object descriptions compared with the age when a sharp increase in self-descriptions occurred.

Subject A's language protocols at 22, 22¾, 23½, and 24¼ months were examined for all words that were predicates or were descriptive of states of objects, because his self-descriptive utterances grew from 5 percent at 23½ months to 15 percent at 24½ months. Initially, he used the word *sit* to describe both the toys he was manipulating and his own behavior, and the words *take* and *stand* to describe other people and toys but not his own actions. He used the word *off* to describe an object and the words *on* and *up* for both objects and the self. Thus, initially these forms were not used only to describe the child's own activity.

A similar analysis performed on Subject E's data revealed that from 17½ months to 19 months, words like *eat, do, cry,* and *sit* were applied almost equally to the self's behavior as to toys and other persons. However, at 19¾ months these words more frequently accompanied the self's actions.

Thus, the first appearance of words like *up, down,* and *more,* which were common bases for coding self-descriptions, was not restricted to descriptions of the child's own activity. But after a few months the children began to use these terms preferentially to describe their own behavior. The children could have continued to describe the actions of objects or of the adults in the room. The fact that they chose to use these words to describe what the self was doing is critical, for it is not obvious, *a priori,* that this function should be enhanced around the second birthday.

It may be that when the child becomes aware of his ability to gain goals through his actions, he feels pressed to comment upon his behavior. His actions have suddenly become a salient incentive for linguistic description, or at least more salient than the activities or qualities of toys or other people. The child does not begin to talk about himself because he can utter verbs, but because he is preoccupied with what he is doing.

The age when each child used *I, we, me,* or her own name in an utterance whose MLU was equal to or greater than 2.0 was noted, as well as when the self was used as either subject or object. All children produced this class of utterance; the range of first occurrence was 19½ to 25 months. Leopold (1939) observed that his daughter Hildegard used "*I* predicate" for the first time at 23 months and used her name for the first time ("Baby Hildegard") at 23 months. And Sully (1896), summarizing the diary data of several writers, suggested that "the great transition from 'baby' to 'I' is wont to take place in favorable cases early in the first half of the third year."

Five of the children in Study 5 produced a sentence in which *I, me, we,* or the child's name was subject, followed by a predicate of action; the range of first appearance was 20 to 27 months. But the appearance of a sentence with the self as agent followed by a predicate describing a psychological state (typically *want, can, can't,* or *like*) occurred after the children had uttered two or three morpheme sentences with a predicate of action. For Subjects E, C, and A this utterance occurred one month later; for L, 4½ months later. For H, both forms appeared on the last visit at 27 months. Only Subject L produced more sentences at 27 months in which psychological state predicates were more frequent than action predicates. But for the majority of children I plus a predicate of action preceded the occurrence of I plus a predicate describing a psychological state. The first use of self-reference occurred a little later in this group of six children than it did in the younger cohort, perhaps because four of the six subjects in Study 5 were selected to be in the early stages of speech development and, therefore, may have been a little slower in the emergence of speech than the middle-class children in Study 1.

In order to determine if the more limited speech protocols gathered in Study 1 were in accord with these results, the first occurrence of self-descriptive utterances for the fourteen children in the younger cohort was examined. Nine of the fourteen produced examples of this class of utterance. The age of first appearance of self-descriptions for these nine children was 16 to 22 months, but the majority (six of nine) uttered their first self-descriptions between 20 and 22 months. The range of MLU when the first self-descriptions appeared was 1.1 to 1.8. This age interval is similar to that reported for the six longitudinal children. Although most children produced their first self-descriptions between 20 and 22 months, two children did so as early as 16 and 17 months. All sixteen children in the older cohort produced self-descriptions. The age of the first self-description ranged from 20 to 27 months, with eight of the sixteen children showing their first such utterance at 20 to 21 months.

Concordance among Variables

The data suggest that during the months prior to the second birthday the six children in Study 5 showed an increase in directives to adults, mastery smiles, self-descriptive utterances, and distress following the model's behavior. Moreover, there was a suggestion of intra-individual concordance among these four measures (see Table 3.3). Because the growth functions for the variables were not linear and the six children differed in their rate of development, it was not obvious which parameter should be selected to reflect each child's rate of growth. The decision to select the age of the first peak value for directives to adults, mastery smiles, and self-descriptive utterances was based on observed correspondences for this parameter within the performances of each child; hence, it capitalized on chance. Age of maximal distress to the model was the time when the child showed the most extreme distress. It referred to the session when the child showed the greatest number of separate behavioral signs of uncertainty, namely crying, clinging to the mother, request to go home, and inhibition of play.

With only one exception (Subject L for mastery smiles), there was relatively good concordance among the times of initial enhancement of directives to adults, mastery smiles, self-descriptive utterances, and maximal distress to the model. The coefficient of concordance (Kendall's W) was $+.62$ ($p < .05$). Further, the period of growth for these four variables was not always in accord with the child's growth functions for MLU. Consider each of the six cases.

Subject E showed a major enhancement in mastery smiles and directives to adults from 18 to 20 months and in self-descriptions from 21 to 23 months, which was the earliest of any of the children. At 21¾, just after the peak of directives to adults and just before the peak of self-descriptions, E showed maximal distress to the model, and at 19¾ months he said his name for the first time. At 21¾ months he produced his first "*I* action predicate" utterance, and at 22¼ months he produced five utterances of the form *I can* or *I can't*. The period from 18 to 22 months is the time when these related functions were being enhanced.

Subject L showed a major increase in directives to adults and self-

Table 3.3. Age when children displayed behavioral indexes of self-awareness (parenthetical number is child's rank on that variable; Study 5).

| Subject | Age (mos.) | | | | Mean rank on 4 variables | Age (mos.) | | |
	First peak for directives to adults	First peak mastery smiles	First peak self-descriptive utterances	Maximal distress to model		First used toy>self as agent in play	First stacked 6 blocks	First self-reference in language
A	22 (3)	20¾ (2)	24¼ (4)	19½ (1)	2.5	19½ (1.5)	20¾ (3)	25½ (6)
T	24¾ (6)	22¾ (4)	23½ (3)	22¾ (5)	4.5	22¾ (6)	22 (4)	24¾ (5)
E	21 (2)	19 (1)	19 (1)	21¾ (3.5)	1.9	21¾ (5)	18½ (1)	19¾ (1)
L	20½ (1)	24¾ (6)	22¾ (2)	20½ (2)	2.8	20½ (3.5)	20½ (2)	20½ (2)
H	23¾ (5)	23¼ (5)	25¼ (6)	23¾ (6)	5.5	19 (1.5)	27 (5.5)	24½ (4)
C	22½ (4)	22½ (3)	24¾ (5)	21¾ (3.5)	3.9	20½ (3.5)	27 (5.5)	22½ (3)
Age Range	20–24¾	19–24¾	19–24¾	19½–23¾		19–22	18–27	19–25

descriptions between 19 and 21 months, and in mastery smiles from 22 to 25 months, about one month later than E. L was the most reserved and temperamentally inhibited child, and it is likely that her timidity made a contribution to the late occurrence of mastery smiles. She was also one or two months later than E in using her name for the first time and in displaying distress to the model. At 20½ months L used her name with an action predicate for the first time, saying, "Do it self" as she was trying to get up on a chair while her mother was attempting to help her. At 22 months L produced her first use of my and her first use of a psychological state word applicable to the self ("sleepy L").

Subject A's language did not become intelligible until 21 months, and the age of peak self-descriptions was delayed until 24½ months, two months after L. But for the nonlinguistic signs of self-awareness, A's protocol was similar to that of E and L. Subject A showed peak mastery smiles at 20¾ months, earlier than L and one month later than E, and showed the first peak directive to adults at 22 months. A's period of enhancement occurred from 20–24 months. He showed maximal distress to the model at 19½ months and a major improvement in memory from 19 to 21 months. At 23½ months he said "my" for the first time, but it was not until 26 months that he said, "Me talk." He provides the best illustration of the gap that is possible between the linguistic and nonlinguistic signs of self-awareness, a 4-month difference between peak mastery smiles and peak self-descriptive utterances.

Subject C was also late in producing intelligible speech. The peak of self-descriptions occurred at 24¾ months. C's period of enhancement was 21 to 25 months. At 22½ months, the time of peak smiles and directives, C used her name for the first time; at 23¼ months she said "mine" for the first time; and at 24 months she used "*I* predicate" for the first time. At 25½ months, after the period of maximum growth in the indexes of self-awareness, she said, "I yad" (meaning "I sad"). At 26 months she said, "It's me, C" and "Do it myself." Thus, 4 to 5 months after the nonlinguistic signs of self-awareness appeared, C produced unambiguous evidence of this competence in her speech.

Subject T showed closer correspondence among the ages for first peak scores for the three variables—22¾ months for smiles, 23½ for self-descriptions, and 23¾ months for directives—but was later in the age when she showed maximal distress to the model—26¼ months. At 22¾ months she used the word "boo-boo" to refer to a variety of norm violations. At 23½ months she said "hard" while solving a puzzle, and at 24¾ months she used her name for the first time. T's period of enhancement was 22 to 25 months, and she was the only child for whom self-descriptions peaked earlier than directives to adults.

Subject H was late in displaying all of the indexes. He showed peak mastery smiles at 23¼ months, peak directives at 23¾ months, peak self-descriptions at 25¼ months, and maximal distress at 23¾. These data argue for the emergence of the functions surrounding self-awareness around 21 to 25 months. H never performed well on the memory test, and he did not show a major improvement in language until the last visit at 27¼ months when he used his name with a predicate of action for the first time.

The mean ranks for the responses suggest that E, A, and L were advanced, T and C were of moderate precocity, and H was growing at the slowest rate for these functions. Directives to adults and distress to the model were better indexes to the mean rank of all variables, perhaps because these two responses are least dependent either on the temperamental disposition to smile or maturity of language. The age when the child first built a six-block tower was also highly correlated with the mean rank on all four variables. This response, too, was not constrained seriously by language or temperament. The building of the six-block tower depends jointly on the child's desire to meet the standards set by the examiner and his expectation of doing so. In a sense, distress to the model is the complement of completing the six-block tower. On the former task, the child knows he cannot meet the standard and withdraws. On the latter, he knows he can be successful and attempts the task.

4

Cognitive Growth

It appears that during the months prior to the second birthday children seem to become concerned with proper and improper actions, and aware of their ability to meet standards of performance generated by the self or imposed by others. If this hypothesis has validity, one might expect a major improvement in performance on intellectual problems set by adults. Once a child recognizes the possibility of correct and incorrect answers, is concerned with avoiding error, and is aware of his ability to solve a problem, he should perform better on cognitive tasks.

The data from Studies 1, 4, 5, and 6 revealed significant improvements with age in performance on the cognitive procedures. But the greatest enhancement of performance typically occurred during the months prior to the second birthday. For example, most children in the younger and older cohorts of Study 1 first became capable of drawing a circle, solving the transposition and relational inference problems, and remembering the location of the prize with eight different receptacles and a 10-second delay around the second birthday.

Memory for Location

The children in Studies 1, 4, 5, and 6 showed major improvements in memory score between 17 and 23 months, the same time when distress to the model and the other indexes of the awareness of standards were growing. Even though the task requirements and materials were probably less familiar to the Fijians than to the Americans, the Fiji children also showed enhanced performance between 17 and 22 months. Thus, by 2 years of age almost all children in the five samples had solved the problem of eight different receptacles with a 10-second delay (see Fig. 4.1; Tables 4.1–4.3). Gellerman's longitudinal

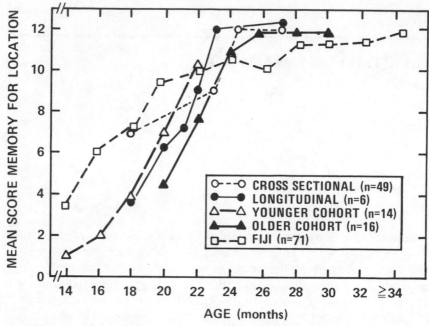

Fig. 4.1. Scores on memory for location test for five samples.

sample of Vietnamese children also showed a dramatic increase in memory performance during the period from 17 to 21 months, with the performance of all five children advanced by 2 to 3 months in comparison with the behavior of the Cambridge samples.

For the younger cohort in Study 1, the improvement was greatest between 17 and 22 months (F for age = 18.56, $p < .001$). By 22 months over 30 percent of the children were able to solve the problem of eight different receptacles with a 10-second delay. Five of the seven boys showed the enhancement in memory before they displayed the growth in MLU, whereas six of the seven girls showed the reverse pattern. Thus, there was no invariant temporal sequence for improvement of memory and speech, even though both competences grew in the months before the second birthday.

Among the older children in Study 1, the age effect was also significant ($F = 38.85$, $p < .001$). One-half of the children, both boys and girls, showed enhancement of memory before MLU; the other half revealed the reverse pattern of growth. No girl in either cohort lagged far behind the other children in either MLU or memory. But two younger and two older boys were several months behind the other children in their scores on the memory task and in MLU.

Table 4.1. Growth functions for selected variables for younger cohort.

Age (mos.)	Average MLU	Memory score	% correct linguistic inference	Trans- position % baby near	Trans- position % daddy near	Trans- position % baby far	Trans- position % daddy far	% solving relational inference (4 correct)	% drawing circle only	% drawing circle and elements	% drawing face
13	<1.0	0.9	0	0	0	0	0	0	0	0	0
14	<1.0	1.0	0	0	0	0	0	0	0	0	0
15	<1.0	1.9	0	7	0	0	0	0	0	0	0
16	<1.0	2.2	14	21	0	0	0	0	13	0	0
17	<1.0	3.2	29	21	0	0	0	0	13	0	0
18	<1.0	4.5	36	29	0	0	0	0	7	0	0
19	<1.0	6.4	57	43	0	0	0	0	7	0	0
20	1.1	7.7	71	43	0	0	0	0	27	0	0
21	1.4	9.4	79	50	7	0	0	0	27	0	0
22	1.8	10.9	79	50	14	7	0	0	53	7	0

Table 4.2. Growth functions for selected variables for older cohort.

Age (mos.)	Average MLU	Memory score	% correct linguistic inference	Trans-position % baby near	Trans-position % daddy near	Trans-position % baby far	Trans-position % daddy far	% solving relational inference (4 correct)	% drawing circle only	% drawing circle and elements	% drawing face
20	1.3	4.3	13	25	6	0	0	0	50	13	0
21	1.4	6.6	13	31	12	0	0	0	75	13	0
22	1.8	9.1	19	50	38	13	13	0	94	19	0
23	2.0	11.0	25	56	44	31	31	13	100	25	0
24	2.3	12.0	31	69	50	31	31	19	100	50	0
25	2.5	13.9	31	69	56	38	38	19	100	56	0
26	2.8	17.0	31	81	69	50	50	25	100	69	0
27	3.1	19.3	31	88	88	63	50	31	100	69	13
28	3.1	19.1	38	88	88	81	63	50	100	75	20
29	3.5	19.5	38	94	94	81	69	56	100	75	20
30	3.6	17.6	38	94	94	88	81	63	100	81	33
32	3.8	18.2	38	100	100	100	88	81	100	94	47
34	4.7	20.1	47	100	100	100	88	88	100	100	53

Table 4.3. Scores on memory for location test.

Age (mos.)	Mean score	
	Study 5	Study 4
17–18	3.5	
18–19	6.3	
19–20	6.8	7.3
20–21	9.0	
21–22	12.0	
22–23	13.6	8.9
23–24	14.1	
24–25	14.7	
25–26	14.7	17.7
26–27	14.7	
28–29	—	12.4

There was no obvious practice effect on the memory score due to repeated visits to the laboratory. At 22 months the younger and older cohorts had similar scores, even though the younger children had nine prior practice sessions at 22 months, while the children in the older cohort had only two earlier sessions. This fact implies that the changes in memory performance were heavily influenced by factors other than familiarity with the materials, examiners, procedures, or testing context. The lack of practice effect was also supported by the scores of the cross-sectional children in Study 4 who were seen on one occasion. These children showed a major enhancement in memory between 19 and 25 months, and there was no significant difference between the longitudinal and cross-sectional samples at any age. At 28 to 29 months about one-third of the children in Studies 1 and 4 had solved the problem with eight different containers and a 10-second delay. The six children in Study 5 showed their greatest improvement between 19 and 23 months, and at 24 months the mean scores were similar to those produced by the older cohort (a mean of 14 for the six longitudinal children and a mean of 12 for the older cohort). However, the final level of performance for the six longitudinal children was not as proficient as it was for the longitudinal samples seen in the laboratory because of the greater number of distractions in the home than in the laboratory. Additionally, the children in the home setting felt less constrained to cooperate with the examiner; there were several occasions when a child simply refused to play the memory game.

Transposition

By 22 months one-half of the children in Study 1 had solved the near transposition problem for "baby," and by 26 months one-half had solved the far transposition problem for "baby" and "daddy." Similarly, the median age of solution of the near problem was 21 to 22 months for the six children in Study 5. The earliest age of solution of the "baby near" problem was 19 months (two children). One child was successful at 21 months, two at 22 months, and one at 23 months. For the daddy near problem the median age of solution was 24 months. Two children solved it first at 23 months, two at 24 months, and one at 25 months. The median ages of solution for the six longitudinal cases and the older cohort in Study 1 were identical: 22 months for baby near and 24 months for daddy near. The Fijian children showed a sharp increase in successful solution of the "baby near" problem from 23 to 30 months; 50 percent answered correctly at 27 months, 3 months later than the Cambridge children (the age effects were significant for all groups).

Drawing a Face

The first attempts to copy the schematic face usually led to a simple scribbling of parallel lines. The next phase was the approximation of a crude circle without any internal elements. The first appearance of a circular form occurred during the middle of the second year, and during the next 6 months most children drew their first circle. In Study 1 all children in the older cohort had drawn a circle by 23 months, and by 24 months half of the older children had drawn a circle with elements (see Table 4.2). In Study 4, 42 percent of the children had drawn a circle by 23 months, and in Study 5, four of the six children had drawn their first circle by 21 months.

The Fijian children's attempts to copy a face were more variable, with the Cambridge children about 5 months ahead of the Fijians (see Figs. 4.2–4.3). This is a larger difference than occurred for memory, transposition, or distress to the model, which suggests that familiarity with crayons and paper may have been a factor in the copying task. Most Fijian families had few books or pictures in the home, and representations of animate forms were rare in traditional carvings or decorations. Further, the word *drawing* is not part of the Fijian vocabulary, and children did not typically have access to pencils, pens, crayons, or paper.

The successful drawing of a circle is probably determined not only by the child's familiarity with the materials and her motor coordina-

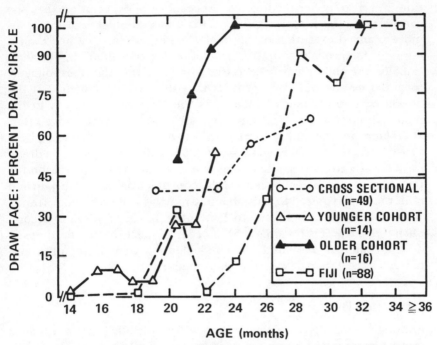

Fig. 4.2. Percentage of children drawing a circle while attempting to draw a face.

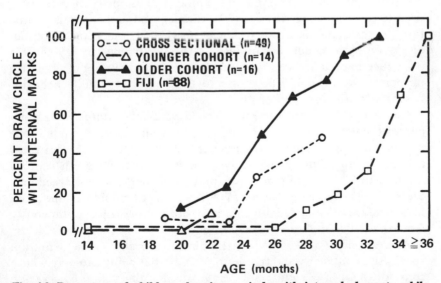

Fig. 4.3. Percentage of children drawing a circle with internal elements while attempting to draw a face.

tion, but also by her mental set, especially the expectation that she can perform the act successfully. This expectation should lead to a more planned execution of the task. Making a circle rather than a straight line probably requires special motor coordination, but additionally, the child must believe that she can draw the more difficult form before she will attempt it. It may not be an accident that the period between 19 and 23 months is the time when distress to the model, directives to adults, mastery smiles, and self-descriptive utterances appear. The ability to place a few dots or lines inside a circle proved difficult, for there was a 4-to-6-month difference between drawing a circle and putting a few lines or marks inside it. The reason for that fact cannot be enhanced motor coordination, since no unusual motor skill is required to scratch a few marks inside a circular frame. Why, then, did it take until 24 to 26 months for the children to accomplish this goal? It is possible that in order to meet the standard posed by the examiner, the child must reflect upon what is required and have an expectation of meeting that standard.

Symbolic Play

Although the tendency to play with toys symbolically is not a response to a problem posed by an adult, it, too, was enhanced in almost all children during the second year. The word *play* is used here in a very specific way. Although play appears as a descriptive category in most treatises on the young child, unlike the majority of categories used by psychologists, it is rarely defined in objective terms. Imitation, for example, is defined clearly as the reproduction of an act displayed by a model; fearfulness as the occurrence of crying or a wary face to certain incentives. But few authors list a set of objective properties that would allow one to decide if the child's behavior belonged to the category of play.

Play is usually defined implicitly as a particular state that accompanies the child's actions. This definition would be acceptable if the private state were potentially amenable to objectification. But most authors writing during the early decades of the twentieth century implied that the state central to play was the "state of freedom." Stern (1930) suggested that play is "free from all outside compulsion; play is neither demanded nor imposed, but bubbles up spontaneously from the individual's deepest craving for action, and its nature, form, and duration are determined by the player himself . . . The definition speaks of spontaneity and freedom . . . Only that being can play whose consciousness is not quite subjugated under the yoke of necessity, under the stress of the struggle for existence" (p. 307).

Koffka (1924) agreed, suggesting that the child is not free in the world of adults and, in play, is removed from that world. Mumford (1925) described play as a preparation for freedom. More modern texts also reflect this view. Hurlock (1975) noted that "play is free and spontaneous and there are no rules or regulations" (p. 76). Hetherington and Parke (1979) stated that play is "the freedom of choice to become engaged in play and to structure or respond to play activities in a highly individual way" (p. 481).

Even Piaget (1951), who usually treated psychological categories in more neutral terms, called play an activity which is "without rules or limitations," and a few lines later inserted the word *free*. Play "freely assimilates things to one another and everything to the ego" (p. 87). After listing four criteria for play, Piaget arrived at a fifth, "freedom from conflicts," which he favored: "Conflicts are foreign to play, or, if they do occur, it is so that ego may be freed from them by compensation or liquidation, whereas serious activity has to grapple with conflicts which are inescapable. There is no doubt that this criterion is on the whole sound. The conflict between obedience and individual liberty is, for example, the affliction of childhood, and in real life the only solutions to this conflict are submission, revolt, or cooperation which involves some measure of compromise. In play, however, the conflicts are transposed in such a way that the ego is revenged, either by suppression of the problem or by giving it an acceptable solution" (p. 149).

It is likely that play has been a popular behavioral category for Western observers of children because it has been regarded, probably unconsciously, as a sign of the metaphysical state of liberty that the West regards as precious. Although we are not opposed to attempts to determine the psychological state the child is in when he is acting, because this information is likely to be of psychological significance, we are relatively certain that the idea that play is an activity which occurs when the child is free of constraints is not theoretically useful. We therefore use play as a behavioral category but make no assumptions about the child's state.

During the first two years of life children manipulate objects, usually the small objects called toys, and their manipulations do not seem to be in the service of biological needs. Prior to the first birthday, these manipulations appear not to have symbolic meaning but rather to derive from the child's motor schemes. During the second year, many of these manipulations are likely to be partial reproductions of responses children have seen adults perform, such as talking on a telephone or drinking from a cup. This class of responses is called symbolic acts.

In Study 1 two variables were coded during the symbolic play sessions with the younger and older cohorts. The first was the percent of time spent in symbolic play, defined as the total time spent in symbolic manipulation of the toys divided by the total time playing. The second variable was the number of symbolic acts and whether or not they were repetitions of a particular act. Both variables were coded separately for the realistic and unrealistic toy sessions (see Tables 4.4–4.5). At every age there were more symbolic acts with realistic than with unrealistic toys, but by 25 months the proportion of

Table 4.4 Growth functions for symbolic play for younger cohort.

Age (mos.)	Symbolic play with realistic toys		Symbolic play with nonrealistic toys	
	% time	No. acts	% time	No. acts
13	5	6.1	1	1.4
14	11	11.3	6	4.3
15	15	11.4	10	3.8
16	19	18.1	8	4.3
17	21	18.7	10	6.2
18	27	16.7	12	4.9
19	24	15.0	13	4.6
20	27	22.0	11	6.6
21	29	26.7	15	7.9
22	31	28.3	16	13.5

Table 4.5. Growth functions for symbolic play for older cohort.

Age (mos.)	Symbolic play with realistic toys		Symbolic play with nonrealistic toys	
	% time	No. acts	% time	No. acts
20	20	20.2	9	5.7
21	25	21.9	17	7.9
22	23	25.9	13	8.2
23	32	26.7	12	7.6
24	30	26.9	19	10.5
25	28	27.2	27	13.6
26	40	26.8	37	17.4
27	37[a]	24.7[a]		
28	30	23.4		
29	25	21.1		
30	24			
32	22			

a. Pooled realistic and nonrealistic toys from 27 to 32 months.

time involved in symbolic play by the older cohort was equivalent with both the realistic and unrealistic toys.

The children displayed more symbolic acts with realistic toys prior to the model's intervention than after it. But when the toys were not realistic, the children issued more symbolic acts after the modeling. This is probably because the children ordinarily did not have many schemes for the unrealistic toys. The model's display of the three acts was an incentive that provoked symbolic play with the less realistic toys.

The growth functions for symbolic play were regular and yielded a significant linear trend with age (see Fig. 4.4). For the younger cohort the age effect was significant for both the realistic and the nonrealistic toys ($F = 4.51$, $p < .01$, $F = 3.46$, $p < .05$). For the older cohort the age effect was significant for the nonrealistic toys ($F = 4.58$, $p < .001$). Finally, the positive relation between number of symbolic acts with realistic and unrealistic toys (the mean across 13 to 22 months for the younger cohort and 20 to 26 months for the older cohort) was stronger for the older than for the younger children (see Fig. 4.5).

The agent. One of the interesting changes in symbolic play during the second year is the replacement of the child with a toy as the active agent in manipulations of objects. One of the most obvious examples was when a child put a toy bottle to a doll's mouth rather than to her own mouth, or placed a telephone beside an animal's head rather than her own. For four of the six children in Study 5 (three girls and one boy), acts in which the self was agent were more frequent than acts in which the toy was agent during the first two to five visits. But by 23 months the latter category either exceeded or was equal to the former for the remaining visits. For these four children the first age when the frequency of use of toy as agent exceeded the frequency of self as agent was 20, 21, 22, and 23 months—the same ages when the other milestones were changing. The remaining two boys (Subjects H and E) never showed a great deal of play in which the toy was the agent. This shift from self to toy occurred at the same age for L and C, at 20 months, although C was not speaking any intelligible language and L was speaking one- and two-word utterances, which suggests that the new response is not dependent upon maturity of speech.

Four of the five Vietnamese children studied by Gellerman first displayed more acts with a toy, rather than self, as agent when they were between 19 and 22 months; in close agreement with the performances of the children in Study 5. Additionally, Fenson and Ramsay (1980), who studied the changes in play over the second year, reported similar results to those of Study 5. Cross-sectional and longitudinal samples of infants at 13 to 24 months were observed in a laboratory

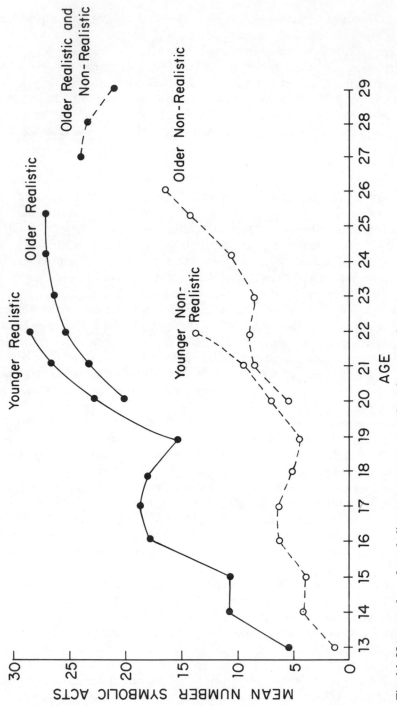

Fig. 4.4. Mean number of symbolic acts across test sessions for two cohorts.

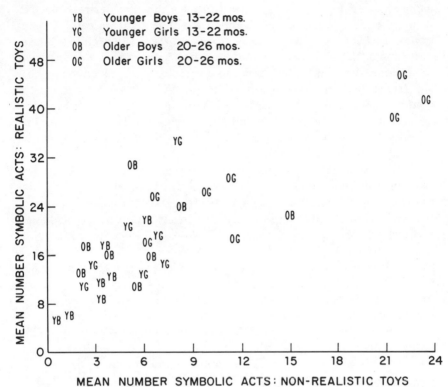

Fig. 4.5. Scatter plot for relation between symbolic acts with realistic and non-realistic toys.

play situation. One of their categories, called "active other-directed acts," was very similar to the response we call "uses toy as agent." They found that the proportion of infants displaying this response increased from 17 percent at 13 months to 71 percent at 24 months, and thirteen of the nineteen children in the longitudinal sample used self as an agent in play several months before they used a toy as an agent; only one child showed a reverse pattern. The increase in this category of behavior was paralleled by an increase in the frequency of acts in which the child combined 2 different responses into a coherent sequence, such as placing a soldier on a platform and then pulling the platform around the room. Such coordinated actions imply an increasing ability to generate a plan and hold that plan in awareness for a period of time.

Largo and Howard (1979) studied cross-sectional samples of children at 3-month intervals from 9 to 30 months of age. The children's play behavior was coded into categories which, though given different names from the ones we used, permitted a division between acts in which the child was the agent, which the investigators called "functional," and actions in which a toy was agent, which they called "representational." The former category reached a peak at 15 months and then declined, whereas the latter category increased in frequency with age. Hence, by 18 to 21 months, actions in which a toy was the agent exceeded in frequency the number of acts in which the self was the agent. Finally, Lowe (1975) found that during the last six months of the second year children began to use the toys rather than the self in pretend acts involving feeding or combing hair.

The remarkable consistency across samples and laboratories in the age when children replace the self with objects in their implementations of symbolic schemes implies a profound maturational change in the mode of object manipulation. One interpretation of this change in play holds that during the second year the child begins to recognize her effectiveness. She has become a director and the toys are her actors and actresses. She puts a doll to bed and tells it to sleep, rather than lying on the toy bed herself. She puts a horse on a truck and takes it for a ride, rather than rolling the truck on the floor. The toys change their role from participants in the child's sensory-motor schemes to symbolic actors in a play the child is both writing and directing. This period is the same time at which the child first whispers to a doll or gives an animal instructions, as if she were manipulating the toy the way adults manipulate her.

Categorizations. During the second year most children spontaneously categorize objects into groups sharing physical or functional similarities. The children in Study 5 typically grouped two or three objects; the most frequent groups included dolls, wooden bowls, plates, puzzle pieces, horses, and cups. The most common dimension of similarity was physical and usually obvious, such as color, size, or shape. Occasionally the groups were pairs of physically different objects that were members of the same functional category, such as edible fruits, animals, or clothing. Placement of the objects together was usually not associated with any verbalization; the child simply placed the objects in a separate location in the room. Although the objects grouped were usually in the child's visual field, it was not uncommon for a child to pick up one member of the category and then search for another until she found it. For example, Subject L, who was holding a toy apple, searched for 20 seconds under a large pile of toys to find some grapes. When she found them, she took the pair of toy fruits to the mother. The fact that this child searched for the second category member suggests that she generated some cognitive representation of the category, and that representation guided the search behavior.

Examination of the individual growth functions for the frequency of categorizations reveals that the two children who were most advanced in speech (Subjects L and E) showed the most categorizations at 18 and 19 months. The three children who were a little less advanced in speech showed a peak number of categorizations at 22, 23, and 25 months, with fourteen, eleven, and ten categorizations respectively. The one child who was slowest in speech development (H) showed no obvious growth function and displayed the fewest number of categorizations. The appearance of categorizations in play preceded the time of the major enhancement in MLU. L and E showed enhancement of speech 1 to 2 months after the visit in which they showed the largest number of categorizations; the frequency of categorizations decreased after that age. H showed six categorizations—a high value for him—one month before a major improvement in his speech.

These data are in accord with similar observations made by Henry Ricciuti (1965). Infants 12, 18, and 24 months old were given objects on a tray (beads, balls, and cut-outs), varying in size, texture, form, and color, while observers coded the children's tendency to touch, manipulate, or group objects sharing dimensions. The most stringent criterion for categorization required the child to place the similar objects in a spatially separate place on the tray. This response showed a major increase in frequency between 12 and 18 months, when about one-third of the sample displayed this behavior.

The detection and occasional generation of a dimension of similarity among objects, whether physical, categorical, or functional, appears long before children note these dimensions in their speech. Once they begin to talk, they will say "two cars" or "another giraffe." Because the child cannot place a person's eyes or shoes on a part of the carpet, she may display her recognition of the category by naming. The linguistic categorizations seem to replace the act of silently putting the two similar objects together, a nice example of the class of change called replacement (Kagan, 1980). The disposition to detect the dimensions shared by events, and to respond to that recognition by grouping or labeling, appears to be a basic process in children. The grouping and labeling may on occasion be epiphenomenal, that is, released by the processes which follow detection of the similarity. Preyer (1889) also insisted that the tendency to form certain categories was innate: "Wordless ideas, wordless concepts, wordless judgments, wordless inferences may be inherited" and "come into existence without the participation of any medium of language whatever" (p. 213).

It is not obvious why the child acts or verbally comments after noting dimensions of similarity. It is reasonable to posit an innate tendency to recognize dimensions of similarity among events. But why does a child act after that private cognitive process? In many cases the child is not trying to communicate any information to another person. The categorization expends energy, yet has no instrumental value, gains no external prize, and is accompanied by no obvious sensory pleasure. Although it is possible that the detection of similarities is accompanied by the generation of a special state of excitement, which in turn provokes the child to do something appropriate, this assumption is attractive only because it satisfies the desire to postulate some "cause" for the act. It is as reasonable to assume that the act of grouping or labeling is performed just because it can be performed, not unlike a well-fed seagull swooping down over a sandy spit just because the spit is there and gulls are capable of swooping.

Imitation

The introduction of the model during the symbolic play sessions provided the opportunity to study developmental changes in imitation during the second year. In Study 1 the major dependent variable was the number of occasions on which a particular act displayed by the model was imitated by the child. Some of these acts may have been witnessed at home and, therefore, might not be imitations of the examiner. An "occasion" was any of the 10-minute periods before or after the model displayed the proscribed actions. That is, an imitative occasion referred to the occurrence of any act displayed by the model during one of the 10-minute segments, either prior to or after the model's demonstration. This variable, rather than the total frequency of imitative acts, was selected because several children stereotypically imitated a particular act ten or twenty times in a 10-minute period. Such large scores would have given a distorted view of the average child's tendency to imitate the model.

Four specific classes of imitation were coded. One was the number of occasions on which the child, during the 10 minutes after the model's demonstration of the three acts, imitated an act exactly as the model had performed it. This was called an "immediate exact" imitation. An exact imitation was one in which the child implemented all the essential actions the model displayed using the same objects that the model had used. This variable was computed for realistic and nonrealistic toys separately and together.

The second class of imitation occurred when the child imitated a fragment of an act during the 10 minutes after the model displayed it, for realistic and unrealistic toys. This was called an "immediate fragmentary" imitation. A fragment was either part of an act witnessed or an act using toys other than the ones the model used. These two variables were called "immediate" because they always referred to the children's imitations during the 10 minutes after the examiner demonstrated them.

The other two types of imitation were called "delayed," whether exact or fragmentary. A delayed imitation was the implementation of a modeled act the child had seen on an earlier visit, whether displayed during the 10 minutes before the model intervened or after. Thus a delayed act was coded if a child imitated an act he had witnessed on a prior day during the 10 minutes before the model intervened or if the child displayed an act during the 10 minutes after the model intervened but the act had not been modeled on that day. Essentially delayed imitations were responses retrieved from the child's long-term memory rather than retrievals of modeled acts witnessed the same day.

Fifty-two percent of all immediate imitations, exact or fragmentary, occurred within 10 seconds of the model's return to the couch, and 79 percent occurred within one minute. But 21 percent of all immediate imitations occurred after one minute, some as late as 8 minutes after the model had completed her performance. The older the child, the longer the delay. The median delay for the 19- to 20-month and 22- to 23-month children was 5 seconds; for the 25- to 26-month-olds it was 45 seconds. In some cases long delays followed an initial period of anxiety; about a third of the children who showed delays longer than a minute showed some form of behavioral distress.

The youngest children, aged 13 to 15 months, were most likely to imitate the basic action displayed by the model, but they often used objects other than the ones she had used, which suggests that the salient schema was for the functional act. After 16 months the children more often selected the exact objects used by the model, and after 21 months they began to create variations on the act modeled, using different objects and modifications of the behavior witnessed.

Among the younger cohort the frequency of occurrence of immediate imitations, both exact and fragmentary, increased from 13 to 14 months and then remained steady until 22 months (age effect was significant at $p < .01$). Exact imitations were a little more frequent than fragments when the acts were relatively simple and could be performed as a unity. However, fragmentary imitations were more frequent at 22 months when the model displayed a new set of more complex acts, presumably because the children had difficulty implementing them as a unity. Delayed imitations also increased significantly with age and were as frequent as immediate acts from 17 to 21 months (see Table 4.6).

Table 4.6. Growth functions for imitation (Study 1).

Age (mos.)	Mean no. immediate exact imitations	Mean no. immediate fragments	Mean no. delayed exact imitations	Mean no. delayed fragments
Younger cohort				
13	0.6	0.3	0	0.1
14	1.3	1.3	0	0.2
15	1.8	1.2	0.2	0.6
16	1.9	1.3	0.6	1.1
17	1.6	0.7	1.4	1.9
18	1.9	0.7	0.6	1.9
19	1.6	1.1	0.6	2.0
20	1.8	0.9	0.4	1.9
21	2.1	1.4	1.2	2.1
22	0.6	2.3	2.4	2.3
Older cohort				
20	2.6	0.9	0.1	0.4
21	2.6	1.6	0.7	1.3
22	0.5	2.1	1.5	2.4
23	0.8	1.8	0.9	2.5
24	0.5	1.6	1.3	3.1
25	0.8	2.3	1.0	2.8
26	0.7	2.5	0.9	2.6
27	0.1	0.7	0.3	2.1
28	0.1	0.7	0.5	2.2
29	0.1	0.7	0.3	1.7
30	0.3	1.1	0.1	0.1
32	0.2	0.8	0.1	0.3

Although there was no relation between frequency of imitations, (pooled for all categories across 13 to 22 months), and memory score, there was a relation between the frequency of imitative acts, immediate or delayed, and the child's MLU at 22 months ($r = 0.6$ with immediate imitations; $r = 0.8$ with delayed imitations). Children with advanced language at 22 months imitated more often during the period 13 to 22 months. This relation did not occur for the older cohort. Finally, for the younger girls there were more exact imitations with the unrealistic toys than with the realistic toys. Contrary to intuition, children under 2 years of age are not more likely to imitate an action performed with realistic than with unrealistic toys, even though they spontaneously play more symbolically with the former.

Among the older infants in Study 1, for whom the acts were more complex, exact immediate imitations were high at 20 to 21 months but declined when the acts became more complex. From 22 to 26 months fragments were more frequent than exact imitations by a factor of 2 or 3 to 1. Analyses of variance revealed that the older cohort displayed more immediate and delayed acts than the younger cohort ($F = 10.39$, $p < .001$ for immediate fragments with realistic toys; $F = 12.64$, $p < .001$ for delayed acts with realistic toys; $F = 9.47$, $p < .01$ for delayed acts with unrealistic toys).

It appears that when the act can be remembered and implemented as a unit, the entire act is modeled. But if the act has several components, the child has difficulty implementing the entire action and will implement a fragment.

Delayed fragments were more frequent than immediate fragments at every age except 20 months, and were more frequent than exact acts from 22 months on, even though there was a positive correlation between immediate and delayed acts ($r = +0.6$). Exact and fragmentary acts were pooled to compare the occurrence of all immediate and delayed acts. From 17 to 22 months for the younger cohort, and from 22 to 29 months for the older cohort, delayed and immediate acts were equal in frequency of occurrence; at some ages, delayed acts were more common. Once a child had seen an act displayed by a model one or two times, the probability of imitating that act a month later was as great as the probability of imitating the same act during the 10 minutes after the model displayed it. This effect was a little stronger when the toys were realistic than when they were non-realistic.

During the second year a child's storage of experience is so well articulated that she is as likely to implement an action seen a month earlier as one witnessed a few minutes earlier. One reason for this fact may lie with the uncertainty over response display, a process that continually monitors the child's action. The child may be too uncertain about her ability to display the observed act immediately after the model. But after the child has had time to assimilate the experience to existing knowledge, she may be ready to implement it.

This result accords with other data. Harnick (1978), for example, divided infants 14 to 28 months of age into three age groups, who then watched a model perform behaviors that were relevant or irrelevant to tasks of varying difficulty. The frequency of imitation of the model was greatest when the task was of moderate difficulty for the child. Thus, for the easiest task the youngest children showed more imitation than the two older age groups; for the task of moderate difficulty the middle infants imitated the most; and for the most difficult task the oldest group of infants showed the most frequent imitation.

Largo and Howard (1979) allowed cross-sectional groups of children 9 to 30 months of age to play with a standard set of toys for 25 minutes.

The play was coded into categories representing different levels of maturity, such as simple exploration of a toy; play in which the child is the agent in a symbolic act; called functional play; and play in which the toy is the agent in a symbolic act, called representational play. Additionally, a model initiated both functional and representational acts and invited the child to imitate her. If the child did not show some representational play in spontaneous behavior, he was unlikely to imitate representational acts that were modeled by the examiner. Further, only the children 12 to 15 months of age who displayed functional play spontaneously imitated functional acts. The authors concluded that acts which are too far beyond the child's understanding or behavioral competence are not likely to be imitated.

These two sets of data provide compelling support for the principle that the probability of imitation is a function of the state of response uncertainty generated in the child. Acts that are too easy or too difficult to assimilate and to perform are not likely to be imitated. These data also contain an important methodological lesson for investigators who study imitation. It may be unwise to limit the period of post-model observation to a few minutes if one wants to make inferences about what representations the child extracted from experience.

Analyses of sex differences in imitation in Study 1, with ages pooled, suggested that girls imitated more than boys for immediate fragments with realistic toys ($F = 4.35$, $p < .05$) and for delayed acts with both realistic and unrealistic toys ($F = 8.29$, $p < .01$ for realistic toys; $F = 13.7$, $p < .01$ for unrealistic toys). These values were based on the means from 13 to 19 months for the younger cohort and 20 to 26 months for the older cohort. But the significant sex difference was due to the behavior of children after 16 months of age, when the acts modeled were more difficult and less feminine in content. When the cohorts were pooled, five of the six children with the lowest imitation scores were boys, and the three children with the highest scores were girls. If the distribution of imitative acts is divided at the median for all children, eleven of the fifteen low imitators were boys, while eleven of the fifteen high imitators were girls (*chi* square = 4.80, $p < .05$). It appears that when girls are calling on their resources for play, they are a little more likely than boys to retrieve acts they have witnessed in others. This disposition has implications for socialization.

A temperamental disposition related to inhibition also seems to be influential in imitation. The boy and girl who were most inhibited in all of the situations, as indicated by playing close to the mother, talking very little, and seeking proximity to the mother when an unexpected event occurred, showed very few delayed acts with either set of toys. The two boys who were least inhibited showed frequent delayed imitations. But this relation did not hold for immediate imitations. It appears that age, nature of toys, sex, and temperament all influence the probability of imitation.

The six children in Study 5 were exposed to different incentives from those in Study 1. The children saw three single acts separated in time and then, after a delay, three acts in succession. Thus, on each visit to the home each child saw six modeled acts in all. We computed the mean number of different acts imitated, whether complete or fragmentary, within 3 minutes following the model's demonstration. The maximum score was 6 (three single acts and the three modeled in succession). Repetitions of a particular act were not scored as imitations. Imitation was least frequent at 17 to 18 months (mean = 1.3); and most frequent at 19 to 25 months (mean = 2.3), the period when the children were showing improvement on the cognitive problems and when their distress to the model was maximal (five of the six children showed maximal distress at 22 to 23 months).

The most comparable data have been reported by McCall, Parke, and Kavanaugh (1977) who had infants 12, 15, 18, and 24 months of age watch models display a variety of actions. Some were motor schemes; others involved social interaction. Some were single unitary acts; others required a coordination of two or more action schemes. These investigators found delayed imitation, implementation of fragments for the acts that had more than one unit, and most important, a major increase in the frequency of imitation after 15 months. Additionally, they reported that inhibited children were least likely to imitate the model. But they failed to find sex differences in imitation. Since their sample sizes were larger than ours, the conclusions from Study 1 should be treated with considerable caution.

McCall and his colleagues interpreted the major change in imitation prior to the second birthday as due to an ability "which permits infants to encode, store, and retrieve an association between two observed entities and to use such an association to guide their own behavior" (p. 26). Enhancement of retrieval memory and the ability to associate symbolic structures were hypothesized as mediating the enhancement of imitation. The increase in imitation after 15 months, in both McCall's study and Study 1, may be due to the fact that the older children feel an obligation to match their behavior to that of the model. If they cannot, they display signs of anxiety, presumably because of failure to meet the standard contained in the model's actions.

Meaning of imitation. Although study of imitation has always been popular among observers of young children, theoretical interpretations of this behavior fall into three historical periods. Nineteenth century writers, of whom Preyer (1888) is an example, viewed the first reliable imitation as an inevitable product of maturation and as the first index of volitional behavior. Imitation represented the dawn of morality, for in this voluntary act the child revealed the capacity to choose to respond: "When a child imitates, it already has a will" (p. 282).

This interpretation changed during the first half of the twentieth century as a result of several forces. First, psychologists began to criticize the lack of specificity, the indeterminacy, and the occultness implied by maturational interpretations. Trying to be faithful to the new demands for scientific objectivity, investigators attempted to externalize the origin of psychological structures. Locke had claimed that all knowledge was derived from sense experience; writers at the turn of the century claimed that new knowledge could also be a product of motor actions. Piaget (1951) argued that the infant's knowledge had its origin in motor schemes that became interiorized.

The mechanism of internalization promised that when methods became more powerful, an investigator might be able to specify the public events that formed the basis for new cognitive structures. The significance of imitation lay in the fact that it was a major source of knowledge: "An idea exists only by virtue of imitation" (Guillaume, 1926, p. 133). One of the most important cognitive structures, a sense of self, was presumed to grow out of imitations of one's own actions: "It is imitation that gradually causes the self to emerge from the unconscious. The first conscious idea will not be that of the self, center of the universe . . . but on the contrary, the notion of an objective self. This objective self is but one unity like all others, since the infant imitates others and achieves self-awareness in so doing" (Guillaume, p. 137).

Unlike nineteenth century observers, Guillaume, Piaget, and their contemporaries were reluctant to treat imitation as an innate disposition. Guillaume assumed that imitation was a competence gradually acquired. Piaget remained an interactionist: "In a word, imitation is acquired through constant assimilation of models to schemas which are capable of being accommodated to them" (p. 82).

Contemporary investigators have returned, in part, to the nineteenth century view of imitation as an inevitable phenomenon, "a capacity that is built into the human species" (Yando, Seitz, and Zigler, 1978, p. 4). Moreover, the imitative act reveals that knowledge was acquired at a prior time; imitation is not the origin of most knowledge, although it can facilitate its retention. There is, however, some remaining doubt over the role of imitation in the creation of new knowledge. Yando, Seitz, and Zigler believe that the reproductive act makes a contribution to the cognitive repertoire, even though it does not have the primacy Guillaume and Piaget supposed.

In less than a hundred years psychologists have come full circle regarding the maturational inevitability of imitation and have created a compromise between Preyer's indifference to the significance of imitation for cognitive growth and Guillaume's faith in its centrality. But no investigator has provided a completely satisfying explanation of the fact that the infant begins to imitate adult behavior by 9 or 10 months of age and with increasing frequency through the second year. The maturational argument assumes that changes in the brain permit the child to use cognitive competences necessary for imitation. One of these competences is the ability to remember what the model did. It is known that retrieval capacity becomes enhanced at 8 to 12 months of age, providing one reason why reliable imitation of a variety of acts does not occur prior to 8 months (Kagan, Kearsley, and Zelazo, 1978). But more than enhancement of memory is needed to explain imitation. For after the child remembers that an adult open and shut her hand, why does he repeat that act? We suggest that events in the environment representing responses which are in the process of being mastered by the child function as incentives that alert or excite the child. The reaction to that excitement is the attempt to reproduce the act.

It is known, for example, that a speech stimulus which engages a schema will lead to babbling in the 8-month-old, and that a visual stimulus which engages a relevant schema will lead to prolonged attention and occasionally a smile. A mother talks with a neighbor, and the child spontaneously repeats some of the words or fragments of words that she hears. Typically, these are words that the child is in the process of mastering, either semantically or phonetically. If hearing the mother talk preferentially provokes vocalization upon cessation of the speech (because the speech engaged in schema), why not assume that perception of an action in another person engages the child's representation of that action? The state produced by the attempted, but unsuccessful, assimilation sets the stage for the action.

The key premise is that representations of an action result in implementations under certain states of excitement. This assumption bothers many psychologists because it contains a mysterious mechanism, namely, an automatic link between representation of an action and its display when the child is in a special internal state. But examples of this principle can be observed in nonimitative contexts during the first 2 to 3 years of life. The 2-year-old sees two pink wooden balls on a carpet amidst twenty other toys, picks up the two balls, and puts them aside, as if recognition of the similarity led to a special state that provoked the child to place the objects together. However, specification of the mechanisms that mediate between knowledge and behavior continues to elude scientists, as it has for centuries.

Interaction with Peers

Unlike performance on the cognitive procedures, most of the variables coded from the peer interaction session of Study 1 did not display obvious growth functions. Moreover, there was a great deal of individual variation in the frequency of various peer directed behaviors and minimal intraindividual stability from month to month (see Table 4.7).

There was much individual variation in the frequency of parallel, or noninteractive, and reciprocal, or mutually interactive, play, with the older cohort engaging more frequently in both behaviors than the younger cohort (see Holmberg (1980) and Eckerman, Whatley, and Kutz (1975) for similar conclusions). Only one pair of younger children showed an obvious increase in parallel and reciprocal play with age. For most of the others the frequency was low. Five pairs of older children showed obvious increases in parallel and reciprocal play, with the main increase occurring in most cases after 26 months. For the remaining three pairs of older children, the frequency of the behavior was low.

As with parallel and reciprocal play, there was a major difference in the frequency of imitation of the peer, with the older cohort imitating much more than the younger cohort. Indeed, no child in the younger cohort showed much imitation of another. In the older cohort, nine of sixteen children showed increases in imitation of the peer with age, and of these, four children showed very frequent imitation. As with parallel and reciprocal play, the major increase in imitation occurred after 25 months.

Table 4.7. Mean scores on selected peer behaviors.

Mean age (mos.)	Offers toy	Parallel play	Reciprocal play	Aggression
	Younger cohort			
13–17	2.8	1.4	0.4	2.8
18–22	1.7	1.3	0.3	2.6
	Older cohort			
20–22	1.3	1.9	0.2	2.2
23–26	1.3	1.2	0.6	2.2
27–34	1.0	3.8	1.2	1.2

The tendency to offer a toy to another child showed the opposite growth pattern. It was more frequent among the younger than among the older cohort and declined with age. Among the older group, only two children over 23 months showed some offering, while among the younger group, nine of fourteen children showed frequent offering (*chi* square $= 8.6$; $p < .01$). However, the tendency to offer objects decreased with time. Since offering is one way to resolve the uncertainty in the interaction, one would expect that as a child becomes capable of predicting the behavior of the peer, uncertainty will become minimal and the offering response will decrease.

Acts of aggression, such as hitting and seizing the property of another child, were more frequent in the younger cohort and a little more common among boys than among girls. For most of the dyads it was not true that one child was always more aggressive than the other. With the exception of one pair of boys, there was no obvious intersession consistency in the tendency for one child to be more aggressive than another. Brenner and Mueller (1980) also reported a decrease, with age, in offering and an increase in aggression in the play of two longitudinal groups of six boys observed for a period of 7 months, from ages 12 to 19 months and 16 to 23 months.

A tentative interpretation of the sequences noted is that initially the unfamiliar child is not a salient incentive for action. As the child approaches the middle of the second year, the peer becomes a more effective incentive, but the child does not know how to interact with the other. In an attempt to deal with the accompanying uncertainty, the child makes overtures as a way to test both the attributes of the other and the child's own power to dominate the situation. As the second birthday nears, the uncertainty is resolved, in part, because the child learns the qualities of the other. The child is now free to enter into play with the other and to use the other as a model.

Language

The speech of the children in Studies 1 and 5 was coded, not because of any *a priori* guesses as to its relation to symbolic play, imitation, or memory, but in the hope of discerning a particular aspect of language growth that would aid in the interpretation of development during the second year. That hope was realized in some small way, for the frequency of self-directed utterances followed closely on the emergence of distress to the model, directives to adults, and mastery smiles. Two additional issues of psychological interest were informed by the protocols. The first pertained to the use of predicates of action and of psychological states. The second involved the relation of language comprehension to both speech development and other cognitive competences.

Unfortunately, the observers in Study 1 did not always record the context of the child's utterances during the monthly play sessions in the laboratory. Therefore, it was not possible to perform detailed analyses of the changing functions of the child's speech, as was done in Study 5. However, some systematic changes were noted in the emergence of predicates and words referring to psychological states.

In the younger cohort in Study 1, thirteen of the fifteen children uttered a total of 103 different verbs, excluding forms of the copula. The majority of the verbs were produced by seven children. Most of the verbs referred to actions and not to psychological states. The children said *eat, play, cook,* and *close* rather than *want, hurt,* or *like.* The major period of enhancement in variety of verb forms was between 19 and 22 months.

Fourteen verbs were used at least once by five or more children:

No. children	Verbs used
5	talk, wash, get, look, move, play, ride
6	come, open
7	eat, sit
8	want, see
9	go

Most of these verbs were spoken by the model during her demonstration of the acts. Only one referred to a psychological state (*want*). Most of these utterances contained the verb without the pronoun *I* or the child's name as agent. The more mature sentence "*I* predicate" was produced by only eight of the younger children. For seven of these eight, this form appeared first between 19 and 22 months. For all fourteen children in the younger cohort two morpheme utterances involving a verb of action occurred before utterances referring to a psychological state. The median age for the first appearance of the former was 19½ months; for the latter it was 22 months and was coincident with the appearance of "*I* predicate." The most frequent psychological state word was *want.* However, *hurt, love, like, feel, try, tired, need,* and *think* were produced by one or two children. These data accord with those of Bloom, Lifter and Hafitz (1980), who reported that the most frequent state words were *want, like, think,* and *feel,* the same 5 predicates that were among the earliest appearing state words for the younger cohort. Bretherton, McNew, and Beeghly-Smith (1981) also reported the appearance of emotional words to describe the self by 20 months of age.

The appearance of these psychological state words represents a special advance in the child's development that has less to do with the growth of syntax than with the fact that the child now has a more definitive representation of her internal states. Of the nine words referring to psychological states spoken by the children on at least one occasion, most appeared between 20 and 22 months (see Table 4.8). The four younger children who uttered psychological state words most often came from the best educated families.

The older cohort in Study 1 generated nineteen different forms describing psychological states. *Hurt, can't, like, need,* and *want* were the most frequent forms. The age of first appearance for most of these words was between 20 and 24 months.

All children in the older cohort used the form "*I* predicate" at least once. The modal age of first appearance was comparable to the

Table 4.8. Occurrence of psychological state words (Study 1).

Verb form	No. children uttering word	Age at first utterance (mos.)
	Younger cohort	
Feel	1	19
Hurt	1	21
Like	2	19, 20
Love	2	21, 22
Need	1	22
Think	1	22
Tired	1	22
Try	2	20, 21
Want	8	18, 19, 21, 22
	Older cohort	
Can	4	23–26
Can't	5	22–26
Could	1	24
Couldn't	1	24
Dream	1	24
Feel	1	25
Forget	2	23–26
Frightened	1	20
Hurt	9	20–26
Know	4	24–26
Like	6	21–26
Love	2	22, 26
Miss	2	24
Need	5	22–26
Remember	1	21
Think	1	25
Thought	1	26
Try	2	21
Want	11	20–26

younger cohort, 20 to 24 months, and thirteen of the sixteen older children first uttered this phrase during that 4-month interval. Of the twenty-four children in both cohorts who generated the form "I predicate," eighteen did so during the period 20 to 24 months. The comparable form "Child's name predicate" showed greater variability in time of first appearance. Thirteen of the older children used their own name, but only six did so between 20 and 24 months.

The age when each child in the older cohort displayed her largest increase in number of different verbs spoken did not always coincide with the time when MLU was growing most rapidly for that child (see Table 4.9). Nine of the sixteen children showed a major enhancement in variety of verbs; for seven of these nine the enhancement did not occur at a time when MLU was growing in a major way.

Linguistic inference. The linguistic inference procedure was de- signed to determine when in the second year children make the inference that an unfamiliar word refers to an unfamiliar object, that is, when they assume that a word they have never heard before has a meaning. Surprisingly, the growth functions for correctly pointing to the unfamiliar object when asked for the unfamiliar word were similar for the younger cohort in Study 1 and the Fijian children. By

Table 4.9. Age of major increase in variety of verbs spoken for older cohort.

Subject	Age at increase in variety of verbs (mos.)	MLU values for months pre- and post-increase in verbs
Girls		
1	25	1.3–1.5
2	—a	—
3	26	2.0–2.3
4	24	1.5–2.4
5	21	1.3–1.3
6	—a	—
7	—b	—
8	—b	—
Boys		
1	26	1.8–2.3
2	—a	—
3	26	1.2–1.3
4	26	1.5–1.6
5	24	1.2–1.6
6	22	1.2–1.8
7	—b	—
8	—b	—

a. No increase.
b. High in variety of verbs at 20 mos.

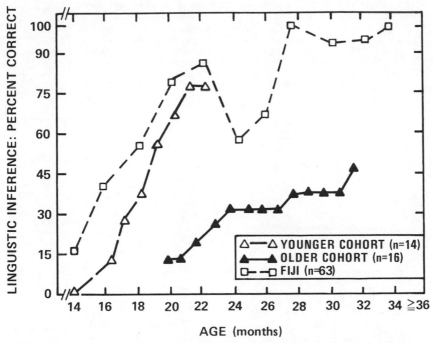

Fig. 4.6. Percentage of children choosing meaningless object in linguistic inference task.

22 months, about 75 percent of both samples responded correctly (see Fig. 4.6; age effects significant). The children in the older cohort did less well, probably because they had more advanced language and as a result assumed that all the objects had a proper name. They behaved as if they did not perceive the article *the* in the instruction, "Give me the zoob." Because they believed that the nonsense syllable was the name of one of the two familiar objects, they often gave the experimenter the doll or the dog and said, "This is zoob." But the similarity in the function for the Fijian and the younger children in Study 1 implies the maturation of a competence that makes the child capable of inferring the name of an object with no prior schemata. Popular theories of language learning assume that the child acquires a vocabulary by direct tutoring and attending to the names people apply to events. But it appears that even before the second birthday children are capable of drawing conclusions about the relation of word to object by cognitive reflection alone.

Language comprehension. The six children in Study 5 were also administered a test of comprehension of simple words. The age was registered when each child successfully answered 50, 75, and 90 per-

Table 4.10. First age of comprehension of word classes (Study 5).

Subject	Age (mos.)		
	50% correct	75% correct	90% correct
	Nouns		
E	19	25	—
L	19	20	21
A	20½	—	—
T	20½	24	—
C	22	24½	25
H	19	20	23½
	Verbs		
E	18	18	20
L	19½	22	—
A	20	20½	—
T	20½	22½	—
C	22	25	—
H	19	21	—
	Modifiers		
E	23½	—	—
L	22	22½	26
A	22	23	25
T	26½	—	—
C	24	27	27
H	22½	25	26

cent of each of the three classes of words probed in the test (see Table 4.10). The age range for comprehending 50 to 75 percent of the words was relatively narrow, compared to the broader age range for a particular mean length of utterance. The language comprehension scores had little relation to maturity of speech production. Subjects E and L were advanced over the other children in mean length of utterance and syntactic complexity, but their comprehension scores were not obviously superior to those of the other four children. Although H's speech remained unintelligible until 21 months, he understood 75 percent of the nouns and verbs by the time he was 21 months old and had comprehension scores better than those of E, whose speech was the most advanced of the six children.

Further, Subjects E and A understood 50 percent of the verbs earlier than they comprehended 50 percent of the nouns, even though nouns were far more frequent in the speech of these children. Four children understood 90 percent or more of the modifiers by 27 months, yet modifiers did not appear frequently in their speech. Thus these data, like those of others (Benedict, 1979), indicate that during the second year comprehension runs ahead of production for both level and growth rate.

Gentner (1978) noted that although 4- and 5-year olds were exceedingly precise in their comprehension of the verb *stir*, (in contrast to *mix* and *beat*) they used the word *stir* in speech production to all three actions: "Paradoxically the verb most narrowly comprehended is the one most broadly produced. This is a rather striking example of the nontransparency in children's word usages" (p. 995).

Commands and imitation of sentences. A second assessment of language comprehension in Study 5, which also involved memory for oral language, required the child to carry out oral commands containing different numbers of units or to repeat sentences of different length. The child's performance was scored for the first age when she reliably carried out two- and three-unit commands and reliably imitated two-, three-, and four-unit sentences (see Table 4.11). With the exception of Subject C, the remaining children carried out two-step units between 21 and 22¾ months, a remarkably narrow interval. Three-unit commands were carried out by five children between 23¾ and 26¾ months—3 months later; only H failed to carry out a three-unit command. Most children had MLU's under 2.0 at the time they were successfully implementing two-unit commands. However, there was not a strong relation between maturity of speech and length of command implemented. Subjects A and T, whose speech was less mature than L's, carried out two- and three-unit commands at the same time as L did. However, E, whose speech was advanced, carried out two- and three-unit commands earlier than H and C, whose speech was delayed.

Although three children successfully imitated three-unit sentences at the same age that they carried out three-step commands, three children imitated four-unit sentences but could not carry out a command with four separate instructions. This is because the units in the commands were less redundant than the units in the sentences to be repeated. The age range for mastery of two- and three-unit sentence repetitions was about 20 to 24 months, the same time when improvement on the other cognitive phenomena occurred. Successful performance on both of these tasks also requires a problem-solving set and a motive to perform with competence.

Perhaps the most interesting finding is that the nature of the predicate was important in successful sentence repetition. All children were able to repeat two-unit sentences with an action predicate 2 months or more before successful repetition of a similar sentence with *want* or *need* as the predicate. That is, the children would repeat "dolly sits" before they could say "dolly wants" or "dolly needs."

Table 4.11. First age of carrying out two- and three-unit commands and imitating two-, three-, and four-unit sentences (Study 5).

			Age									
			Imitated sentences									
			Action predicate			Want as predicate			Need as predicate		
Subject	Carried out 2-step commands	Carried out 3-step commands	2-unit	3-unit	4-unit	2-unit	3-unit	4-unit	2-unit	3-unit	4-unit
L	22	26	19¾	20½	22	21	21	22	21	21	22
E	21	23¾	21	23¾	23¾	23½	23½	24½	23½	23½	24½
T	22¾	25½	22½	26	—	—	25	—	26	—	—
A	22	24¼	22	24	—	22½	—	25	22½	25	25
C	25	26¾	25	—	—	—	—	—	—	—	—
H	21¾	—	26	—	—	—	—	—	27	—	—

Admittedly, the three action verbs were intransitive, while the psychological state verbs were transitive, which may have led the children to expect an object to follow the verbs referring to state. Further, even though the word *want* was much more frequent in the children's speech than the verb *need*, it was not always imitated earlier. These data suggest that one potentially sensitive way to assess completeness of comprehension of a word is to determine when the child will successfully repeat that word in a sentence.

The language data affirm the suggestion made by others (Brown, 1973; Bloom, Lifter, and Broughton, 1979; Clark, 1979) that the child's speech grows from nonintelligible vocalization—which can be communicative, epiphenomenal to states of excitement, or expressive of frustration and desire—to intelligible utterances which name objects, qualities, places, or states; communicate desires; request information; express affect; describe the actions of self, objects, or people; and maintain conversation. The language data are also in accord with the prevailing view, as well as opinions held in the nineteenth century, that most of the time a concept is already established in the cognitive repertoire before it is expressed in speech (Bloom, 1970, 1973; Macnamara, 1972; Nelson, 1974; Cromer, 1974; Slobin, 1977).

The nonlinguistic signs of awareness of standards and one's ability to meet them appeared in all children between 19 and 23 months. Self-descriptive utterances usually occurred after these nonlinguistic signs. For Subjects E and L, the two children with advanced speech at 19 months, self-descriptions and use of self-reference occurred only a month after the appearance of the nonlinguistic signs. But for the remaining four children, for whom intelligible speech was slower to appear, self-descriptions appeared several months later. This division between linguistic and nonlinguistic evidence of self-awareness was especially characteristic of Subject A.

Awareness of one's standards, states, intentions, actions, and competences are nonlinguistic constructs. To assimilate the feeling of fatigue to a prototypic schema created in the past and to recognize that this state is associated with sleep does not require language. When the child learns the word *sleepy*, he may label his state. Similarly, language is not necessary to generate the idea of "being on mother's lap" and to initiate an appropriate response to gain that goal. When the child learns the word *up*, he may say it. But although words describing actions usually appeared after single nominals, this does not mean that the young child has no schemata for action. Similarly, action words almost always appeared before words descriptive of psychological states, but it is not obvious that ideas of action are articulated before ideas representing psychological states.

Although absence of language cannot be used to infer absence of a relevant psychological idea, some investigators hope it might be possible to use sequences in speech to diagnose sequences in the establishment of a set of psychological concepts. For example, "*I* action predicate" typically occurs before "*I* psychological state predicate." It is tempting to infer from this fact that these two ideas are also established in that order. But given the available evidence, one cannot assume that the sequences in speech parallel the order of establishment of comparable ideas. As Goldin-Meadow, Seligman, and Gelman (1976) noted, one cannot infer comprehension from production data or productive knowledge from comprehension data.

Early speech development presents at least three distinct phenomena requiring explanation: the reasons for the first appearance of speech, the bases for the orderly sequence of semantic classes, and the growth of syntax. These are different phenomena probably requiring different solutions. The appearance of speech requires first that the child appreciate that heard words represent established schemata. The linguistic inference data on the younger cohort imply that before the middle of the second year most children appreciate that speech refers to events in the real world. In addition, in order for speech to appear, the child must be able to retrieve a linguistic form that has become associated with a schema. Most important, there must be an incentive to release the spoken utterance, such as excitement, response uncertainty, desire for a material goal, or communication. During the second year children often use the active naming of objects as alternatives for manipulating them (Nelson and Bonvillian, 1973).

The order of appearance of semantic classes has attracted far less attention than the growth of syntax. The first words typically refer to objects in the immediate field, usually smaller than the child and capable of movement, most often animals, parts of the body, food, and clothing. This fact does not necessarily indicate, however, that the child's first ideas are for these objects. The presence of an incentive is likely to be a critical determinant of the sequence of semantic classes in speech (Braine, 1974). Objects that are slightly discrepant from the child's knowledge comprise a primary class of incentives because they generate a state of uncertainty. The first modifier terms used by children 24 to 30 months of age are typically used to name discrepant events: "Most of the words used in this form are those describing a transitory state of an object or person. The are used, that is, primarily as descriptive adjectives to talk about a within object change" (Nelson, 1976, p. 28).

Perhaps one reason the child's first spoken nouns are usually names of toys, rather than names of pieces of furniture in the room, is that top replicas are discrepant transformations on regular forms, not that they are manipulable (Nelson, 1973, 1974). This idea is in accord with the suggestion by Greenfield (1979) and Greenfield and Zukow (1978) that reduction of uncertainty is an important determinant of the word selected by the child. According to Greenfield, the child is likely to utter a word that will be most informative: "Informativeness is used in the information theory sense of uncertainty . . . the concept of informativeness will be used to predict when the child will encode the object verbally and when he will encode the change of state" (p. 160).

Greenfield suggested that uncertainty is increased when an object is not in the child's possession. When the object is undergoing a process or state change, the process rather than the object becomes more uncertain and, hence, is more likely to be described. Thus, when a child hears a car outside, she says "car." But when she pushes a toy car, she is more likely to say "bye-bye."

In addition, the discrepancy principle may contribute to the early appearance of plurals in the child's speech. Most of the child's experience consists of nonidentical objects. The close spatial proximity of two identical shoes, cups, or eyes is uncommon and, therefore, discrepant. The child is attracted by such events, creates an idea of "twoness" or plurality early, and is prepared to learn the proper morpheme and use it when he sees a pair of cups or shoes. This suggestion does not deny the potential importance of Brown's (1973) suggestion that the perceptual salience of a spoken morpheme is also a determinant of the order of acquisition.

Although discrepancy seems to be a useful principle in explaining why some words appear earlier than others, it is obviously not the only—or even the central—principle. Additionally, the child is sensitive to opposites and contrasts. Soon after *up* and *big* appear in speech, the American child begins to say the pairs *up/down* and *big/little* in close temporal succession, as if the child's mind is attracted to events that share many features but differ maximally in one central dimension.

The appearance of words describing the self and its actions—even before MLU 2.0—requires yet a third principle. The 2-year-old has matured to a point where she is aware of her ability to effect change and to inhibit or to initiate an action. This awareness recruits the child's attention to her actions, and as a result, cognitive representations of her behaviors become conscious. The typical 15-month-old is unaware or far less aware of her behaviors. Even though she may comprehend some verbs and may use action words to describe the movement of toys, she does not use the same predicates to describe her own activity. It is not the lack of availability of predicates that prevents her from labeling her own behavior but, rather, the fact that her activity is not yet an idea that she reflects upon and evaluates. This may be one reason that there is a delay between the availability of nouns and verbs in the child's receptive vocabulary and the appearance of three- and four-morpheme sentences which describe the child's activity.

Goldin-Meadow, Seligman, and Gelman (1976) suggested that, "the developmental delay between vocabulary production and length increases in our longitudinal study indicates that a relatively large store of productive nouns and verbs is not sufficient to bring about increases in utterance length" (p. 197). They noted that vocabularies of the period before and after the increase in length of utterance are qualitatively different. One potential basis for this difference is that the older child begins to talk about himself.

Many reports and essays on child language begin with a set of *a priori* categories that parse the child's language into classes which take their direction from linguistic analyses of adult language: "Children develop certain conceptual representations of regularly recurring experiences and then learn whatever words conveniently code or linguistically represent such conceptual notions . . . Thus, it is only coincidental that in the adult model, *see* and *stop* are verbs; *there* and *away* are adverbs and *up* is a preposition. Children learn to talk about the experiences of the world; descriptions of the words that they use in terms of adult parts of speech are superficial and misleading" (Bloom 1973, 112).

It is potentially useful to categorize the child's speech in accord with the state and intention of the child. Admittedly, these two qualities are difficult to infer, and as long as they resist reliable classification, they lie outside science. But suppose, for the moment, that one could make valid inferences of intention or state for children's utterances. Under these more hospitable conditions, a useful category for children's speech might be "communications that announce a desire for an object." Now the noun *cookie*, the verb *want*, the deictic *there*, and the adverb *up* (while the child climbs up on table to get a cookie) would all be placed in the same category.

During the early phase of speech, immaturity of syntax does limit the range of the meanings a child can express. But when the child has become capable of three- and four-morpheme utterances, he has the ability to talk about a variety of topics. The fact that the 2-year-old talks about his behavior and intentions cannot be explained by an appeal to more mature syntax. There is also maturational constraint on the diversity and complexity of motor acts. The 8-month-old can perform a limited set of actions with his hands, while the 30-month-old can initiate a greater variety of complex motor movements. But at 3 years, when the child can implement a variety of acts, some are far more frequent than others. The hierarchy of acts displayed is not explained by maturation. One must know the child's intentions. Although the child at the one-word stage cannot describe his emotions due to maturational limitations, at age 3 years, when he can express many ideas, the selectivity of his utterances referring to emotions cannot be explained by noting that the child has the ability to produce sentences with more complex syntax. Although the focus here is on the child's intentions in classifying his early language rather than on formal grammatical classes, both classification schemes are of theoretical significance.

The parsing and description of phenomena and the selection of constructs to name covariation among phenomena are two seminal issues in all empirical science. The category "self-descriptive utterances" referred to only one aspect of the child's speech, ignoring all others, and was invented *a posteriori*. The two-morpheme "Fix it" could have been spoken while the child was manipulating a toy, pointing to a toy on the floor, or watching an adult fix a small object. Thus the utterance could have been classified as an action sentence, a declarative sentence, a sentence with a pronoun, a request, the naming of an event, or a self-descriptive utterance. The category chosen depends on the investigator's theory and purposes.

Relations among Domains

A final result of interest is the relative independence of the variables quantified in Studies 1, 4, and 6, especially the lack of a strong relation between maturity of speech and the nonlinguistic cognitive performances as the children approach their second birthday. Although there was suggestive, intra-individual concordance in Study 5 for the age of appearance of maximal distress to the model and the first peak for directives to adults, mastery smiles, and self-descriptive utterances, the more popular question concerns the concurrent correlations among levels of performance during the time a set of competences is being enhanced.

A critical decision is the selection of the ages to sample performances. In Study 1 a conservative strategy was adopted; namely to select the age when all children were displaying the response in question. Because the main focus was the relation of MLU to the other variables, it was necessary to use MLU at 22 months for the younger cohort, inasmuch as some of the younger children were not speaking at the earlier ages. That decision necessitated the use of the memory score at 22 months, which was not a problem, because all children were solving some items on the memory problem at that age and there was considerable variability in performance at 22 months. The average score was computed for symbolic acts, imitation, and distress to the model across the interval 18 to 22 months because the score for any single age was low and variability was seriously restricted.

For the older cohort it was possible to sample at several ages. The primary basis for selection was variability. Thus MLU was assessed at 22, 26, and 34 months; memory was evaluated at 22 and 26 months. But by 34 months most children had solved the most difficult memory problems, and therefore variability was seriously restricted. A similar rationale held for relational inference, transposition, and drawing (see Tables 4.12–4.13 for intercorrelations among these variables).

There was greater independence among the cognitive variables for the older than for the younger children. For example, among the younger children, MLU at 22 months was significantly related to memory at 22 months ($r = .59$, $p < .05$), mean number of symbolic acts from 18 to 22 months ($r = .66$, $p < .01$ for realistic toys; $r = .56$, $p < .05$ for nonrealistic toys), and delayed imitations from 18 to 22 months ($r = .65$, $p < .01$). Additionally, the memory score at 22 months was associated with the number of symbolic acts with the nonrealistic toys from 18 to 22 months ($r = .67$, $p < .01$). Among children who had just begun to speak, the level of language development tended to covary with a variety of cognitive performances. But 7 months later, when all the children were speaking, the variation in spoken language was more independent of variation in other cognitive capacities.

Among the older cohort, MLU and memory were not related at 26 months, and neither MLU nor memory assessed at 26 months was significantly correlated with any other cognitive variable. With the exception of a positive relation between the scores on the transposition task at 26 and 29 months and the maturity of drawing a face at 34 months, there were no significant correlations among the cognitive scores after 22 months of age. The relative independence of language, memory, relational inference, maturity of drawing, transposition, and symbolic play imply different rates of growth for the cognitive processes underlying these competences in a 2½-year-old.

When the data from the younger and older cohorts in Study 1 were pooled at one age, 22 months, there was relative independence among the variables, although language and memory were associated ($r = .66$), and symbolic play with realistic and nonrealistic toys

Table 4.12. Intercorrelations among selected variables for younger cohort.

Variable	1 MLU (22 mos.)	2 Memory (22 mos.)	3 Drawing score (22 mos.)	4 No. symbolic acts (18–22 mos.) Realistic toys	5 Nonrealistic toys	6 Mean no. imitations (18–22 mos.) Immediate	7 Delayed	8 Mean no. distress to model realistic toys (18–22 mos.)	9 Mean score parallel play with peer (18–22 mos.)	10 Mean no. offers to peer (18–22 mos.)
1	—	.59a	.25	.66b	.56a	.49	.65b	.33	−.03	.21
2		—	.15	.26	.67b	.34	.24	.67b	.53a	.05
3			—	.06	.00	.39	−.19	−.20	.26	−.11
4				—	.54a	.63a	.44	.00	.03	.38
5					—	.52a	.39	.63a	.45	.38
6						—	.40	.01	.50	.52
7							—	.20	.00	.53
8								—	.10	−.20
9									—	.47
10										—

a. $p < .05$
b. $p < .01$

Variable	1	2	3	4	5	6	7	8	9	10	11	12
	MLU			Memory		Relational inference	Transposition		Drawing score			Mean no. distress to model realistic toys (20–26 mos.)
	22 mos.	26 mos.	34 mos.	22 mos.	26 mos.	29 mos.	26 mos.	29 mos.	26 mos.	29 mos.	34 mos.	
1	—	.88b	.64b	.76b	.45	.49	.28	.15	.13	.39	.19	.20
2		—	.88b	.63b	.38	.47	.29	.27	.08	.46	−.02	.11
3			—	.43	.27	.34	.11	.22	.00	.39	−.03	.27
4				—	.59a	.21	.01	.04	−.02	.17	−.02	.28
5					—	.05	.03	.29	−.07	.02	.00	−.06
6						—	.35	.28	−.13	−.11	.41	−.15
7							—	.62a	.06	.33	.61a	−.28
8								—	−.09	.32	.52a	−.14
9									—	.48	.17	−.20
10										—	.01	−.03
11											—	−.07
12												—
13												
14												
15												
16												
17												
18												
19												
20												
21												
22												
23												

13	14	15	16	17	18	19	20	21	22	23
Mean no. distress to model nonrealistic toys (20–26 mos.)	Mean no. immediate imitations — 20–22 mos.	Mean no. immediate imitations — 23–26 mos.	Mean no. delayed imitations — 20–22 mos.	Mean no. delayed imitations — 23–26 mos.	No. symbolic acts realistic toys — 20–22 mos.	No. symbolic acts realistic toys — 23–26 mos.	No. symbolic acts nonrealistic toys — 20–22 mos.	No. symbolic acts nonrealistic toys — 23–26 mos.	Mean score parallel play with peer (27–34 mos.)	Mean score imitation of peer (27–34 mos.)
−.12	.11	.13	−.14	.36	.14	.37	.09	.34	.05	.03
−.29	.08	.16	.09	.39	.33	.44	.27	.40	.08	.30
−.41	.10	−.23	.19	.12	.11	.13	.19	.03	−.05	.16
.03	.06	−.05	−.10	.16	−.01	.27	−.07	.18	.18	.01
−.24	−.09	.11	−.18	−.01	−.15	.08	−.05	.13	−.07	.01
−.48	.01	.52[a]	.10	.57[a]	.40	.36	.38	.48	−.17	.02
−.28	.07	.26	−.21	.30	.05	.32	.07	.28	.21	.29
−.65[b]	−.04	.52[a]	.11	.36	.04	.43	.26	.39	.15	.11
.01	.75[b]	.15	.15	.24	.37	.03	.54[a]	.37	−.05	−.33
−.28	.21	.08	.21	.26	.06	.23	.32	.43	.53[a]	.31
−.29	.20	.39	−.15	.22	−.04	.20	.06	.15	−.18	−.52[a]
.07	−.13	−.54[a]	−.21	−.23	−.44	−.24	−.49	−.44	−.25	−.22
—	.18	−.42	−.05	−.16	.01	.02	−.31	−.27	.19	−.16
	—	.08	.33	.50[a]	.46	.30	.57[a]	.35	−.13	−.44
		—	.34	.66[b]	.56[a]	.55[a]	.64[b]	.78[b]	.13	.00
			—	.59[a]	.71[b]	.50[a]	.73[b]	.52[a]	.39	.11
				—	.73[b]	.79[b]	.75[b]	.86[b]	.24	.05
					—	.52[a]	.86[b]	.68[b]	.24	.09
						—	.46	.78[b]	.35	.17
							—	.77[b]	.18	−.02
								—	.34	.19
									—	.51
										—

a. $p < .05$.
b. $p < .01$.

showed a positive correlation ($r = .42$). Only one association held for both cohorts: the number of occasions of distress following the model's actions with the realistic toys (across the period 18 to 22 months in the younger cohort and 20 to 22 months in the older cohort) was correlated with memory performance at 22 months ($r = .67$, $p < .01$ for the younger cohort; $r = .46$, $p < .10$ for the older cohort).

The major scores for the primary variables assessed in Study 4 were also intercorrelated both for all children and for the two older age groups separately. The memory score was more highly correlated with language comprehension ($r = .44$) than with mean length of utterance ($r = .19$) (see Tables 4.14–4.15). Because the age differences in language and performance on the other tests were so large, and transposition, drawing, and relational inference did not begin to improve until 25 to 26 months, the intercorrelations among these variables for the two older age groups (25 to 26 months and 28 to 29 months) were examined separately. MLU and language comprehension were positively correlated, but relational inference, transposition, and drawing a face were generally independent of each other and of MLU. Among

Table 4.14. Intercorrelations among major variables (Study 4).[a]

Variable	Relational inference	Draw a face	Trans-position	Memory	Language comprehension	MLU
Relational inference	—	57[b]	.08	−.14	.47	−.22
Draw a face	−.29	—	.39	.63[b]	.53	.48
Transposition	.01	.25	—	.41	.55[b]	.57[b]
Memory	.33	−.23	−.12	—	.43	.23
Language comprehension	.34	.20	.17	.35	—	.55[b]
MLU	.36	.32	.05	.17	.60[b]	—

a. 25- to 26-month-olds to the right and above the diagonal; 28- to 29-month-olds below and to the left of the diagonal.
b. $p < .05$.

Table 4.15. Intercorrelations among four major variables for all 49 children (Study 4).

Variable	Age	MLU	Language comprehension	Memory
Age	—	.72[a]	.56[a]	.18
MLU			.62[a]	.19
Language comprehension				.44[a]
Memory				—

a. $p < .01$.

the three children with the highest memory scores, one solved the relational inference problem, two solved transposition, and one drew a face. However, the ten children who drew the most mature faces had memory scores that were not different from those of the children who did not draw a face. Thus, as with the longitudinal data in Study 1, there was not a strong relation among the performances across the varied procedures.

The Fijian data of Study 6 also revealed relative independence of the major cognitive variables for each of five age periods (16 to 19 months, 18 to 21 months, 22 to 25 months, 23 to 26 months, and 27 to 30 months). There were no statistically significant correlations among the scores for memory for locations, linguistic inference, drawing, transposition, and occurrence of distress to the model at any of the five age periods. Additionally, neither ordinal position, size of household, level of parental education, nor indexes of family wealth showed consistently significant relations with performance on the test procedures.

Both the Fijian and the Cambridge data argue against the idea of a unitary change in cognitive competences during this developmental era. The specificity of growth for cognitive talents should not be surprising, because different classes of cells, tissues, and organs also grow at their own characteristic rates, which vary with genetic constitution, state of differentation, and local environmental conditions. As Weiss (1968) noted, "mode and rate of growth of each cell type are specific for that type" (p. 260). Cognitive competences, too, have to be regarded as specific in origin and in rate of developmental enhancement. The organization and growth patterns of mental functions are no less differentiated than the biological structures from which they are ultimately derived.

5

Attempt at Synthesis

During the last half of the second year the child displays for the first time a preoccupation with adult standards, affect appropriate to successful and unsuccessful mastery, directives to adults to change their behavior, and language that is descriptive of the child's actions. Although these phenomena do not reflect one overarching function, they may be related. More important, the similarity in age of onset and era of growth of these reactions, among and within the various samples, implies that these diverse phenomena are likely to be consequences of maturational changes in the central nervous system in children growing in any environment with people and objects.

The data do not announce an obvious organizing idea; hence, any selection must be tentative. It is possible to impose coherence on a portion of the corpus by hypothesizing several functions that monitor development during the second year. But we explicitly reject a concept, like "developmental rate" or "developmental level," which applies to all major cognitive functions during an era of growth. Such general constructs—g being one example—are not theoretically useful and are not in accord with the relative independence we found among many of the indices of cognitive development.

The central psychological victories of the last half of the second year appear to include both the appreciation of standards and the emergence of awareness of the self's actions, intentions, states, and competences. The word *standard* refers to a cognitive representation of an external event, action, or internal state which the child regards as proper, or ethically good, although not necessarily motivationally desired. Therefore, the child experiences an obligation to attain or maintain that representation through action or thought, and is emotionally aroused by a violation of that representation. *Self-awareness* refers to a set of psychological functions which evaluate the child's states, thoughts, and behaviors, and his ability to meet standards. Self-awareness is not a single explanatory entity; but a semantic convenience to unite different, but related, functions. As Eddington (1928) remarked, "Some name for the coherences in nature is always useful. The contemplation in natural science of a wider domain than the actual leads to a far better understanding of the actual" (p. 266).

Other investigators may prefer a different name. Our use of the word *self-awareness* is motivated by the behaviors that were changing during the last half of the second year, namely mastery smiles, directives to adults, anxiety to the model, and self-descriptive utterances. Self-awareness is only a summary term implied by those behaviors and not an explanation of them. We do not declare that the 8-month-old is not aware that she is hungry. This last statement should not be taken as announcing a sudden timidity over our conclusions. Quite the contrary. The use of the construct *intelligence* to summarize a set of responses to the Wechsler Intelligence Scale for Children does not have the same meaning as the intelligence that describes a 6-year-old's correct solutions to a series of conservation problems. Similarly, the use of *anxiety* to explain or describe the increase in frequency of distress to unexpected events across the period from 7 to 15 months of age is not the same anxiety inferred from the increase in phobias among 4-year-olds. Bridgman (1958), commenting on the Heisenberg uncertainty principle, noted, "It is well recognized that there is no sharp dividing line between the instrument of knowledge and the object of knowledge, and that for different purposes the line may be drawn at different places" (p. 62). If the psychologist's procedures are substituted for "instrument of knowledge," then what may appear as timidity becomes a principle of understanding.

Words used as constructs have meaning only with reference to a specific set of data. For example, Weiskrantz (1977) showed that the truth value of statements describing the cross-modality matching ability of monkeys (haptic to visual) depends on the procedures used by the investigator. The monkeys fail on some procedures; they succeed on others. Similarly, the validity of statements about the degree of human amnesia following bilateral removal of the hippocampus depends on the specific memory probes employed.

Further, propositions about the perceptual salience of particular stimulus dimensions for infants, like the size or distance of a particular object, must add a statement describing the child's prior familiarity with the object. Groups of 6-month-old infants were habituated on one of two three-dimensional representations of the human head (large or small) at one of two distances. All groups were dishabituated to the same head, which differed in size, distance, or both dimensions from the habituated standard. The largest increase in attention occurred among the children who were exposed to a head that was changed in size, rather than in distance from the child. But when the same procedure was implemented with cubes rather than heads, the increase in attention to the transformed stimulus was much smaller in magnitude, and the largest gain in fixation time was displayed by those children who were exposed to a change in distance, not size. Thus it is usually not possible to make universal statements about the salience of size, distance, color, or shape; the salience of any dimension is specific to the procedure that generated the data (McKenzie, Tootell, and Day, 1980).

The meaningfulness of heritability also depends on the context of evaluation and the age of the subject. Observers rated the behaviors of children from a large longitudinal sample of identical and fraternal twins, while each was being administered the Bayley Developmental Scale at 3, 6, 9, 12, 18, and 24 months. Factor analyses of the ratings revealed that the second factor was best described as a disposition to fearfulness and inhibition—a quality that may have biological roots (Kagan, Kearsley, and Zelazo, 1978). However, the identical twins had significantly more similar ratings on this dimension only at 6 and 24 months, not at the other four ages (Matheny, 1980). This apparently odd profile of coefficients becomes reasonable if it is assumed that the display of fearfulness is a function of cognitive maturation and the nature of the incentives. It is possible that the incentive of an unfamiliar examiner is especially potent at 6 months, the time when stranger anxiety begins, and the incentive of potential task failure is especially potent at 24 months of age, due to the growth of self-awareness. These incentives actualized the children's biological vulnerability to inhibition. Evidence for heritability of this property was absent at the other ages because the appropriate incentives were not administered. The statement, "Fearfulness is heritable during the first two years of life," is misleading; the scientist must append to that conclusion the context of measurement and the developmental stage of the subject.

This is not an idle issue in the social sciences. There is far greater consensus among physicists and chemists than among psychologists over the methods appropriate to particular descriptions or theoretical statements. When a chemist writes about the acidity or temperature of a solution, his colleagues know and agree on the selection of the evidential source of that statement and appreciate the relation between the observation and the construct. For controversial classifications, like "particle," the physicist is careful to tell his colleagues whether his observations came from a Wilson cloud chamber or a linear accelerator, for the meaning of *particle* is not identical in these two procedures.

Psychologists, however, work with far less agreement than physical scientists and, unfortunately, with less concern over the degree of consensus regarding the relation of a classification construct to its source. Psychologists argue, for example, about the effect of surrogate care on the infant's attachment to its caretaker. One reason for the controversy is an indifference to the fact that some investigators use behavior generated in the Ainsworth Strange Situation as the measure of attachment; others use clinging to the mother in the home; and still others use separation anxiety. Since these procedures do not produce theoretically equivalent behavior, statements about an infant's attachment do not have the same meaning. Similar criticisms hold for conclusions about memory, imitation, motivation, affect, and a host of other psychological terms.

When we say the child develops self-awareness between 15 and 23 months, we refer to the growth of a very specific set of behaviors. Other observers have used different names for the psychological changes that characterize this era of growth. Tiedemann (1787) remarked that the child develops *Eigenliebe* (love of self) during the same period; the Utku of the Hudson Bay believe the child develops *ihuma* (reason); and Preyer (1888) suggested that *Ichheit* (selfhood) emerges during the second year.

Important premises are hidden in each of these phrases. Although Tiedemann and Preyer assumed that the behavioral changes indexed a new appreciation of individuality, the Utku, like most non-Western societies, emphasized the child's ability to appreciate the difference between right and wrong (Briggs, 1970). It is understandable, after the fact, that urban Europeans would wonder about the origins of the narcissistic, autonomous, and actualizing ego, while small, isolated, hunting or agricultural communities would be more concerned with the child's adherence to social norms. The name chosen for a complex phenomenon has connotations for empirical work. If the complex event that genticists call "mutation" had been named "replacement," "alteration," or even "damage," different experiments might have been performed. Self and self-awareness are very popular ideas in the West; hence, the contemporary scholar's mind leaps to these words quickly. If these same data had been discovered by a seventeenth century Chinese observer, he would doubtless have used a different term. Thus Paul Weiss's (1968) comment on the use of the term *growth* is appropriate for self-awareness: "Growth is not a simple and unitary phenomenon. Growth is a word, a term, a notion, covering a variety of diverse and complex phenomena. It is . . . a popular label that varies with the accidental traditions, predilections and purposes of the individual or school using it" (p. 241).

Normative Standards

Some time during the second year the child displays obvious concern with a special class of events or personal actions whose attributes deviate from what adults regard as normative. The behavioral index of concern is typically a pointing to the discrepant event, accompanied by a dysphoric vocalization, serious facial expression, and on occasion, the morphemes "oh, oh." It is important to differentiate between this class of deviant event and the majority of other discrepancies the child encounters. The state created by noting an event discrepant from a previously established schema, such as the mother's wearing a large red feathered hat, is qualitatively different from the state generated by noting a discrepant event, like a dirty shirt, that has been associated with a form of adult disapproval. Although the feathered hat and the dirty shirt are discrepant from normative experience, the latter is a violation of a standard; the former is not. A dirty shirt is not only a discrepant variation on the more frequent phenomenon of a "clean shirt"; it is also an event which the child has linked with behavior that signifies adult displeasure.

It is important that our observations indicated that the children showed signs of displeasure or apprehensive concern only to a small class of discrepancies, namely those that violated adult standards, like dirty clothing, broken toys, regressive behavior, improper attire, illegitimate foods, and toileting accidents. All of these are more likely to be associated with adult displeasure than are equally discrepant events, like a new piece of jewelry on the mother, a fold in the carpet, or a rearrangement of furniture. Because most discrepant events detected by the child passed without comment, it is theoretically useful to assume that a special class of discrepant events has been linked to signs of adult displeasure.

How does the child learn which events violate normative standards? During the second year the standards center on cleanliness, the integrity of property, harm to others, and toileting. It is unlikely that all children will decide by 18 to 24 months that a dirty blouse is a violation of a norm; they must first be exposed to some information which leads them to classify certain actions and their associated outcomes in a special way. The most likely possibility is that certain events provoke special adult reactions which generate a state of uncertainty in the child. These adult reactions can be as subtle as an unexpected change in the timbre of the parent's voice or the shape of her eyes, or as salient as a verbal reproof or a spanking. The associations among the event (the norm violation), the unexpected parental reaction, and the subsequent state of uncertainty lead the child to award salience to the violation. Interviews with the Fijian parents revealed that the two most frequent behavioral categories regarded as "wrong" (*cakava cala*) were the destruction of property and acts potentially dangerous to the child's physical welfare. Aggression was the third most frequent class of disapproved actions.

Initially the association is probably between a class of actions with associated outcomes (spilling milk on a shirt or pulling a curtain down) and the emotional state of uncertainty over adult reactions. The one- to two-year-old's natural tendency to create categories for events that share properties and to infer their cause results, in time, in the establishment of a special class of outcomes whose common characteristic is the fact that production of any member of this class is capable of generating a special form of uncertainty. Representations of these classes of outcomes and their complements are standards. When the child learns the words *bad* and *good*, she will apply them to these classes of events.

The child probably does not have to be "punished" for every violation. Because 18-month-olds generate prototypic representations of events, detect deviations from those prototypes, and react to the detection, there is reason to believe that they are able to generate the idea of an improper event, or violation of a norm. Although it is more parsimonious to assume that children must experience a "punishment" for every action-outcome they will classify as a standard, it is not beyond credibility to suggest that once children have acquired some information about the undesirable nature of certain action-outcome pairs, they will "go beyond this information," as they did in the linguistic inference task, and spontaneously generate schemata that represent appropriate states and their contrasting violations. One 2-year-old in Study 1 became visibly upset because she had a small doll and a large toy bed and could not find a small toy bed, which she indicated was more appropriate for the doll. This action implies that 2-year-olds are prepared to impose an evaluative dimension on experience. What is required for the actualization of this disposition is a level of cognitive maturity, attained during the second year, and experiences that permit the children to associate some events with signs of adult displeasure. These can include disapproval for soiling, breaking a glass, or tearing a shirt. These experiences may create a sensitivity to all events that violate adult norms, especially those that might have been produced by the actions of a person. Many of the children studied commented on a slight, almost invisible, crack in one of the toys which in no way affected the toy's function, but they never commented on a crack in the paint that covered the door of a cabinet in the playroom. They would comment on a ragged hole in a piece of cloth but not on a smooth hole in a piece of wood. The incentive for the comment on the cracked toy was not the fact that it was a discrepancy, but that it was seen as a violation of a normative state which might have been produced by someone's behavior.

Certain of the competences that mature during the second year might permit the child to become aware of standards on behavior. Obviously, she must be able to recall that certain action-outcome sequences provoke signs of parental displeasure. But the ability to recall the past was present much earlier. Clearly, comprehension of the mother's verbal communications about an action facilitates acquisition of the standard. Here, too, there is evidence suggesting that by 13 to 14 months most children have some initial understanding of adult speech.

We suggest that a new function which emerges by 17 months is a tendency to infer the cause of an event. The child now expects events to have antecedents and automatically generates cognitive hypotheses as to cause. The data from the linguistic inference task indicated that by 17 months most children infer that an unfamiliar name must apply to an unfamiliar form. Wachs and Hubert (in press) found that age changes in performance on the Piagetian scales of infant development reveal a major increase in foresight between 18 and 22 months of age. To this new function must be added the prior experience of parental disapproval of acts that violate the normative state of objects. Hence, when the child sees a crack in a toy, he infers the crack was caused by someone's action. Because that class of actions is associated with adult disapproval, he responds affectively. The child is said to have a standard for the destruction of property when he has a representation of classes of acts which violate the integrity of objects and are associated with adult disapproval. The ease with which the child associates signs of disapproval with actions suggests he is prepared to construct that link. Perhaps one function of the infant's dependence on adult care, which most suppose to have an adaptive purpose, is to make the growing child attentive to the caretaker's behavior and to prepare him to react with a state of uncertainty when the caretaker raises her voice, frowns, strikes the child, or otherwise reacts in ways that are unexpected.

The possibility that during the second year children become prepared to evaluate actions and events as good or bad because of their potential to produce uncertainty has an analogue in the hypothesis that species differ in their biological readiness to associate classes of stimuli. Rats are prepared to associate gustatory stimuli with unpleasant, visceral states; birds are prepared to associate visual stimuli with those internal states. This line of argument, which implies that young children move into an evaluative set toward the end of the second year, is affirmed by interviews with the Fijian mothers, who commented that children naturally become more responsible after their second birthday when they have acquired *vakayalo* (sense). As a result of this new competence, parents begin to hold children more responsible for their actions. The recognition by the Fijians of a sudden appreciation of right and wrong is in accord with the belief of nineteenth century observers that young children are innately moral.

James Sully (1896) suggested that the child has an "inbred respect for what is customary and wears the appearance of a rule of life" and an "innate disposition to follow precedent and rule, which precedes education" (p. 280–281). For "there is in the child from the first a rudiment of true law abidingness . . . the day when the child first becomes capable of this putting himself into his mother's place and realizing, if only for an instant, the trouble he has brought on her, is an all-important one in his moral development" (p. 289–290). Sully believed all children must, because they are human, realize that causing harm to another is immoral. Such knowledge can never be lost, regardless of any subsequent cruelty the child might experience. Therefore, the child does not have to learn that hurting others is bad; it is an insight that accompanies growth.

In a popular text written at the turn of the century, Tracy and Stimpfl (1909) asserted that the child is born with a disposition to be moral: "Moral ideas do not require to be created or implanted in the minds of children by their elders. Nothing is more certain than that the child is born potentially a moral being, possessing a moral nature which requires only to be evoked and developed by environmental conditions . . . If no amount of training can ever make a moral being of a dog, it is because he possesses no moral nature to begin with. If a child is capable of attaining to advanced moral ideas and distinctions, it is because he possesses at the outset a moral nature upon which instruction and discipline can take hold. An empirical account of the derivation of the moral nature out of conditions in which no germs of it are to be found, fails utterly when tested by observed facts or by logical criticism" (p. 179).

This interpretation of the young child's concern with standards is favorable to some of the premises of sociobiological theory, for it implies that appreciation of standards and their violation is an inevitable event in ontogeny. It even suggests one of the advantages that might accompany early actualization of this competence. Because humans have the capacity for enduring resentment toward persons and desire for personal property, together with the ability both to plan and to plot in order to attain these goals, it may have been necessary in human evolution to make sure that early in development inhibitory functions would emerge to curb these disruptive dispositions. An appreciation of proper and improper behavior should facilitate the inhibition of aggression to siblings, especially to young infants. The importance of inhibition of aggression to younger children is reflected in a rare event noted in a San Francisco newspaper (December, 1980), the killing of a 22-month-old by a 30-month-old peer who was his regular playmate: the aggressor pounded the victim's head on the floor and struck his skull with a heavy glass vase. But the recognition that one's behavior might deviate from a standard should also lead to an inhibition of attempts to solve problems and to deal with challenges that potentially might be within the child's sphere of mastery, as in distress to the model. Hence, timidity may be the price one pays for socialization of disruptive acts. Some might argue about the relative advantages of withdrawal in a mastery situation compared with voluntary checks on aggression. But both properties may be packaged as a unit, and the child cannot have one without the other.

Mastery Standards

A second phenomenon of the second year is the occurrence of a smile while the child is pursuing or after she has attained a goal in solitary play, as in building a tower, putting a final piece in a puzzle, or fitting a dress on a doll. Shinn's (1907) diary revealed many observations of a young child who showed enormous delight in autonomous mastery during the second year: "a noticeable trait was the child's interest in doing something novel with her body, apparently in mere curiosity and sense of power" (p. 371). The 12-month-old also smiles to moderately familiar events and plays without interruption for many minutes. But the 12-month-old is less likely to show the sequence of: selecting an activity with a goal without an obvious incentive present, persisting in attempts to gain that goal despite difficulty, and smiling upon the goal's attainment. Additionally, although the 12-month-old cries if someone interrupts her play or takes an object from her, she does not usually cry when she is unable to complete a goal-directed sequence because of insufficient ability. The 18-month-old does. These two complementary and developmentally novel phenomena—the smile to success and the distress to potential failure—require the positing of a second class of standards.

During the last half of the second year the child is able to maintain self-generated goals in awareness while she invests effort in trying to attain them. The representation of a goal to be attained through effort can also be regarded as a type of standard, but the representation is not a discrepant variation on the normative prototype. Second, the representation has not been associated with signs of parental displeasure. Nonetheless, the child feels she "should"—is obligated to—attain the goal through action.

It seems useful, therefore, to posit one class of standards, called "normative," which contains representations of actions and events that have been linked with adult approval and disapproval. The familiar list of aggression, destruction, and cleanliness is prototypic. The second class, called "mastery standards," contains representations of goals to be attained through actions that have not necessarily been associated with adult displeasure or praise. We recognize that we are reinventing the distinction between the two components of the Freudian superego: the violations of a community's values and the representations that define the ego-ideal. We did not have that distinction in mind as we studied the children's behaviors; the data invited the distinction. For both types of standards the child must maintain articulated representations of goals over time without incentives in the immediate field.

Finally, unlike the infant under one year, the 2-year-old is aware of her ability to meet the standards she generates. If there is moderate uncertainty generated by the relation between her competence and the goal, the resulting state often leads to action. But action is less likely if she does not have the competence or if the goal is met too easily. The incentive for action now includes uncertainty over attaining a representation of a goal, in addition to the uncertainty over assimilating an event into a possessed schema. The 18-month-old lives with both stimulus and response uncertainty. Traditional theory has held that initially the child learns what external events and actions are proper by observing adult behavior; only later does she incorporate these beliefs into a set of internal standards. These data suggest that once the child is mature enough to generate a goal she is able to meet, typically during the second year, she feels obliged to meet it. Robert White would call this phenomenon "effectance."

Two-year-old children begin to show resistance to coercion and a desire to implement actions without interference from others. This latter behavior, which nineteenth century parents called "willful," may reflect the fact that the child is trying to meet standards of competence in domains where adults intervened in the past. The child's desire to feed herself cereal with a spoon may be no different in mechanism from the desire to build a tower of six blocks. In both cases the child is generating a standard to be met. In the former, parents interfere and try to feed the child; they do not interfere with the building of the tower. As a result, the child is regarded as willful when she feeds herself cereal, but not when she is building a tower of blocks.

The "terrible two's" is a consequence of the fact that the child is aware of the standards set by parents and she tests their validity in order to reduce her uncertainty over the degree to which they will be enforced by adults. These actions are not always in the service of rebellion or hostility. They are simply an attempt to gain knowledge that will provide the child with a more exact definition of the standard and its breadth. Once that knowledge is gained and the uncertainty resolved, the child becomes more serene and less mischievous.

A mother who was a subject in one of our longitudinal investigations reported that her 2-year-old boy dropped some recently ironed clothes into the toilet. When the mother discovered the act, her anger, exacerbated by the heat of the day and the time it took to iron a pleated skirt, led her to strike the child with an intensity far in excess of her normal behavior. The child cried for a very long time and seemed to the mother to be very frightened. Several days later, the boy repeated the act with a new stack of laundry. But this time he immediately came to the mother, told her what he had done, and stiffened his body as if to accept a spanking. This second mischievous action seeemed not to be in the service of hostility but rather to determine if the serious punishment experienced several days earlier was, indeed, caused by his prior action. This time the mother did not strike the son; she told him why such behavior was annoying. He apparently never did it again.

Self-Awareness

A third competence that seems to emerge before the second birthday is awareness of one's feelings, intentions, actions, and most important, competence or lack of competence to attain a goal defined by a standard. The critical observation that led to this conclusion was the display of distress to the model's actions which appeared in all the samples. The distress occurred because the child accepted the model's actions as a standard, but was aware he could not meet that standard. At least three significant pyschological functions must emerge, in sequence, during the period from 12 to 24 months of age, in order to create the conditions necessary for this behavior.

The first function, which appears just before or soon after the first birthday, is the ability to treat objects as symbols. By that phrase is meant that the child treats one object as a sign or subsitute for another. The child can impose a meaning or function originally acquired in the context of one object on a quite different object.

The second function appears a few months later when the child is able to treat the speech of others as representative of objects and events. This advance is somewhat more mysterious than the earlier one, for the relation between the spoken word and its referent is more arbitrary than is the referential relation betwen one object and another, as when a piece of cloth is treated as a blanket. The child in the second year expects that events have meaning, where meaning is defined as the cognitive representation of a coherent set of reactions, whether behavioral, affective, or cognitive, linked to and potentially provoked by an event. Some time around the first birthday, and certainly by 18 months, the child becomes prepared to treat an envelope of sounds as a sign. Although animals can be taught to treat an object as a sign, the child seems to go further and to change psychological frames. The 6-month-old selectively attends to an event's physical qualities—its size, orientation, color, pattern, light intensity, and arrangement of elements. But during the second year that conceptual set becomes subordinated to a different cognitive orientation. The child now appreciates that objects and actions have names and functions. Events have a meaning which transcends them. Because the child assumes that events have both names and a purpose, he is prepared to inquire, privately, about the names of new objects he encounters and the significance of events. Major support for this claim comes from the children's performance on the linguistic inference task, where the 16- to 18-month-olds assumed that the unfamiliar form must be named by the unfamiliar word. Regardless of whether or not chimpanzees can be taught a form of language, no one has claimed that language-trained chimpanzees spend a large part of their day inquiring about the names of new objects, and spontaneously signing those objects whose "names" they are in the process of acquiring.

The disposition to impose meaning leads a child to assume, for example, that an odd-looking piece of scrap wood on the floor has a function and a name. If the child sees her mother perform an action for the first time, such as watering a plant, she may be prone to inquire privately about the aim and purpose of the action. If a stranger enters the room, the child assumes that the adult has a name and that her actions have a purpose which is potentially knowable.

The third significant psychological function involves the appreciation that names and actions that deviate from a norm are incorrect or improper. Evidence for this conclusion comes from the fact that the 18-month-old begins to laugh at incorrect names and, more important, at discrepant behavior that he initiated, not just at discrepant behavior produced by another. A one-year-old laughs if an adult behaves in an unusual way, such as making the sound of a cow, but the one-year-old does not generate his own violation of a norm and then laugh. Additionally, the 18-month-old shows concern with events that violate norms, inhibits actions prohibited by the parents, and displays behavioral signs of apprehension, or at least wariness, when initiating a sequence that violates a prohibition, as when he approaches cautiously an expensive vase his mother has told him not to touch.

It is now possible to interpret the phenomenon of distress to the model. The child watches the model, creates a schema for her actions, and automatically inquires into the meaning of the model's behavior. The child asks privately, "Why is she doing that? What is the event called?" as he will ask about the name of a photograph of an animal mounted on the wall of a room. One answer to the private inquiry is the assumption that he should—is obligated to—implement the model's behavior. When an adult leaves the chair she is sitting on, sits down beside the child, and initiates a coherent action, the child is disposed to assume he should repeat those actions. If he cannot, either because the act is too difficult or the child forgot it, signs of distress may appear. But how does the child "know" he cannot repeat the modeled act before he even attempts to do so? In order to explain the distress, it is necessary to assume that the child has some awareness of his competence to meet the standard implicit in the model's action. If he has only moderate uncertainty over meeting the standard and there is a possibility of being successful, he will make an attempt —a state illustrative of Plato's axiom, "To know the good is to do the good." But if the child believes that he cannot implement the proper action, he becomes vulnerable to distress (the children in Study 3 who displayed some imitation of the model were least likely to show distress).

A few months later children will verify this chain of assumptions in their speech. The 26-month-old will say, "I can" or "I cannot do that." Children now set themselves difficult problems and draw adult attention to their products because they want others to notice they have met the standards they have generated.

After observing that the emergence of self-consciousness and morality develop gradually out of observation and imitation of others, James Mark Baldwin (1897) turned to the phenomenon of bashfulness, which he saw as innate and "a differentiation of animal fear"

(p. 199). He suggested that the bashfulness which occurs in the second year is due to the fact that the child has become self-conscious about his behavior: "These exhibitions of organic bashfulness are modified as soon as the later development of self-consciousness brings in reflective modesty" (p. 200). Baldwin accepted the self-consciousness of the second year as a fact and used it to explain inhibition and anxiety. We first noted anxiety to the model and inferred self-consciousness.

Romanes (1889) devoted an entire chapter to self-consciousness, asserting that although young infants have no self-consciousness, heredity guarantees that all will develop this function. He postulated a basic as well as a more advanced form of self-consciousness. The former, which is possessed by both animals and men, refers to the recognition of one's actions and feeling states: "Outward self-consciousness, then, is the practical recognition of self as an active and a feeling agent, while conceptual or inward self-consciousness is the introspective recognition of self as an object of knowledge and, therefore, as a subject" (pp. 199–200).

Because Romanes viewed language, especially the appearance of the pronoun *I*, as the platform upon which self-consciousness is built, he placed the emergence of self-consciousness much later than we do and made language a more essential catalyst. When the child begins to talk, "as yet there is no inward self-consciousness but only outward: as yet the child has paid no attention to his own mental states, further than to feel that he feels them; and in the result we find that the child speaks to himself as an object, i.e., by his proper name or in the third person. That is to say, the child does not yet set himself in opposition to all outer objects, including all other persons, but regards himself as one among many objects. The change of a child's phraseology from speaking of self as an object to speaking of self as a subject does not take place—or, but rarely so—till the third year. When it has taken place we have definite evidence of true self-consciousness, though still in a rudimentary stage" (p. 201).

Preyer (1888) anticipated much of our data and essential conclusions when he suggested, based on detailed observations of his son over the first three years of life, that during the second year, "The child wants to manage for himself without assistance, to pull, push, mount, climb, water flowers, crying out repeatedly and passionately, 'Ich mocht ganz alleine', (I want to do it alone) (p. 185). Preyer called this state the "I"-feeling and argued that the experience of pain is necessary for the emergence of self. He described how his son gradually recognized parts of his body and began to grimace at himself when he saw his reflection in the mirror. Preyer realized that this "I"-feeling occurs prior to the use of any personal pronoun or any indication of a concept of self in the child's language: "The wide-spread view that the 'I'-feeling first appears with the beginning of the use of the word 'I' is wholly incorrect . . . These observations plainly show that the 'I'-feeling is not first awakened by the learning of words, for this feeling, according to the facts given above, is present much earlier; but by means of speech the conceptual distinction of the I, the self, the mine, is first made exact; the development, not the origin, of the 'I'-feeling is simply favored" (pp. 202–203).

Preyer believed not only that experience causes changes in the central nervous system (anticipating modern neuroscience), but also that increasing numbers of sense impressions gradually lead to "a continually increasing growth of the gray substance of the child's cerebrum, a rapid increase of the intercentral connecting fibers, and through this a readier co-excitement—association, so called—which unites the feeling with willing and thinking in the child. This union is the 'I,' the sentient and emotive, the desiring and willing, the perceiving and thinking 'I' " (p. 207).

There is persuasive evidence for the 2-year-old's ability to appreciate and recall some of his perceptual and feeling states. Novey (1975) visited children 18, 27, and 36 months of age at home and invited them to play with either a pair of ski goggles that permitted vision or a pair that was opaque and gave a sense of blindness. A day later each child came to a laboratory setting and, after a period of play, watched the mother put on the opaque goggles. The 27- and 36-month-olds who had had previous experience with the opaque goggles behaved as if they inferred that their mothers could not see. They tried to remove the goggles, asked the mother to remove them, and made fewer gestures toward her, in comparison with the children who had been exposed to the transparent goggles. The behavior of the 18-month-olds was no different under the same two conditions.

Longitudinal observations provided by mothers specially trained to record their children's reactions to the distress of others revealed a major change in behavior during the latter half of the second year. The children now behaved as if they were inferring the state of the victim, and accordingly, they issued appropriate responses. They hugged or kissed the victim, gave him a toy or food, and requested aid from an adult. Those behaviors were absent or infrequent to the same incentives during the early months of the second year (Zahn-Waxler and Radke-Yarrow, personal communication).

These data indicate that by or very soon after the second birthday children are capable of inferring a psychological state in another person, based on their prior experience, which implies that they can recall their earlier perceptual or affective experience and act on that information. It does not seem too bold to add that these findings imply that the children are now conscious of their experience.

The increasing frequency of directives to the mother between 19 and 24 months seems understandable if we assume that one reason the child begins to order the mother around is that he has some expectation that the adult will conform to his instruction. Although the 6-month-old cries when hungry, cold, or in pain, it is unlikely that he is aware of the relation between the cry and the goal he wants, or has any firm expectation regarding the effectiveness of his cry. But when the 19-month-old shoves a puzzle piece in front of his mother's face and whines, we submit he is aware of the relation between that action and the goal and anticipates that he will be helped.

Once the child becomes aware of his capacity to generate goal-directed actions, the probability of their overt display is a function of the child's expectancy of attainment—an assumption readily accepted for adult functioning. When some 20-month-old children say, "Hard do" while working on a difficult task, it is tempting to award them some awareness of their ability to attain a goal.

Persuasive support for the positing of self-awareness is seen in requests to the mother to repeat an action the child has just completed. Similarly, when the 2-year-old smiles after putting her whole hand into her mouth, bangs her head, runs upstairs after being told not to, pretends to eat her mother's fingers, puts a toy pitcher on her head, combs her hair with a toy broom, puts on her mother's shoes, feeds a toy animal a screwdriver, refuses to conform to her mother's request, crawls under the sofa, or makes her finger urinate into a toy toilet, it is difficult to resist awarding the child some awareness of what she is doing.

We treat smiling in these situations as an index of self-awareness, but do not do so when the 4-month-old smiles to a familiar face or voice. The key difference between the two smiles is that the smile of the 20-month-old follows an action that met or violated a standard, such as solving a puzzle, producing a discrepancy, labeling an object, or getting a parent to conform to her request. The child does not smile at all actions aimed at a goal; indeed, she smiles at only a tiny proportion of her goal-directed actions, namely those that recruited a special affective investment. Because the 10-month-old is unlikely to smile after what appears to be similar investment in a goal-directed action, it is reasonable to suggest that the smile of the 2-year-old reflects the fact that she is aware of the goal she was seeking and therefore of her success. Attainment of the goal releases the smile. The smile to an outcome event produced by the self after the investment of effort, rather than to an external source, invites the speculation that the child is continually aware of the goal event being sought. If she were not, then when the goal was attained, she would not know she had generated it and would not smile. Thus, smiling following one's own goal-directed behavior can be treated as evidence for awareness of one's behavioral intentions.

The appearance of utterances that describe the child's own actions provide the least ambiguous evidence of this construct. The child's first one-word utterances refer primarily to objects and to desires. But by 20 months a new function emerges without a major increase in length of utterance. The child begins to describe her own behavior. As she turns a lid on a jar, she says, "Turn" or "Fix." As she lifts herself onto her mother's lap, she says, "Up." The 20-month-old has many other topics she could describe. She could have described the actions of the mother, but she does not. She could have commented on changes in sounds in her environment; she does not. She could have described the dynamic motions of milk, juice, or water, or the colors of her clothes. But she chooses none of these. Rather, she begins to describe her own actions and intentions and, 2 to 4 months later, her psychological states. This class of utterance appears to reflect the fact that awareness of one's capacity to effect change has become salient because it is a novel psychological state, not unlike the 4-year-old who hurriedly tells her parents about a novel experience she has just had.

Speech corrections made by 2-year-olds can also be regarded as evidence of an aspect of self-awareness. Clark and Andersen (1979) reported on the spontaneous corrections that 2- and 3-year-old children make in their speech. A 28-month-old said, "I *mood*—I *move* it." These corrections, called "repairs," are phonological, lexical, and syntactic, and they imply an awareness of what one is saying. The authors suggested that such repairs by children are "strong evidence they are aware of language . . . Without the ability to monitor, check, and then repair one's utterances, it is unclear how children go about changing a rudimentary system into a more elaborate one."

During the first stage of speech, when excitement is one significant incentive for talking, the affect generated by recognizing an object whose name the child knows almost reflexively provokes a verbal description. During the early period of observation in Study 5, from 17 to 19 months, the child was affectively aroused by external events, typically objects whose names he was in the process of acquiring. The source of the affective arousal lay with the external incentive. The child's play at this time was not consistently planful but continued to be controlled by objects he happened to notice or events he recognized. The child's behavior had not yet come to be guided more regularly by his own ideas. But as the child moved closer to the second birthday, his behavior became more planful: he saw a puzzle to solve and resisted distractions, or he went to his bedroom to retrieve a toy. The appearance of directives to the mother also reflects the fact that once the child generates the idea of a goal, he does not lose that representation. It stays in awareness; hence, the child asks a familiar adult for help in attaining a self-generated goal. A few months earlier the goal would have more quickly disappeared from awareness.

As the ability to generate ideas of goals and to hold them in awareness is enhanced, the child comes to have his next insight. He becomes aware of the fact that he can initiate, cease, and monitor his actions. That fresh realization is as affectively arousing as the earlier recognition that objects have names, and so the child starts to describe what he is doing. The child finishes a puzzle and declares, while clapping his hands and smiling, "I put it on." He searches for a toy, pauses, and as he runs to his room, declares, "I know where my puzzle is," and then, moments later, "I am throwing my puzzle downstairs." He laughingly repeats a half-dozen times, "I am stepping on my ankle," presumably because the self-reflexive meaning of the seentence is interesting. Like twoness and holes in pajamas, the awareness of one's capacity to act recruits attention, and the child describes what he is doing in whatever words are available. A few months later, descriptions of the self's psychological states will appear, and finally, statements about the child's ability. By 27 months the child has offered enough evidence to conclude that he is aware of his behavior, intentions, and psychological states and of his ability to monitor and implement them. In a more traditional idiom, he has self-consciousness, which seems to be composed, in part, of standards and an awareness of whether he can meet them.

Spemann's concept of organizer has metaphorical value in this discussion. The awareness of one's qualities, competences, and ability to affect others may act as an organizer, leading to new and special interpretations of experience. Now, but not before, children treat symbolic communications about their behavior as reflective of the self. Once a child becomes conscious of the self as an entity with potentialities that are evaluated on a good-bad dimension, experience takes on a different significance.

By 24 months the two precocious children in Study 5, Subjects E and L, were beginning to show evidence of a new set of competences. The observers noted a decrease in inhibition and timidity, an increased persistence in play, a more playful attitude with toys (L said, while holding an animal over a toy toilet, "Maybe her foot like to pee"), and most important, more frequent role playing. The children pretended they were babies or adults or posed a question to their mothers the way adults present questions to them. At 27 months, E made a whirring sound with a toy airplane and asked his mother, "What's that, Mommy?" When she answered correctly, he smiled. Later in the hour he brought a toy giraffe to one of the examiners and asked, "What's that?" in a tone, voice, and posture of interrogation, and then answered himself before the examiner could reply. At one point, after tossing an orange in the air, he asked the examiner directly, "Can you do that?"

Sensitive parents have also noted that the child becomes less irritable, less prone to fear, and more spontaneous after 2 years of age. The increased spontaneity seems to occur because the child becomes more firmly aware of her ability to deal with uncertainty and is better able to control her anxiety. Distress to the model, anxiety with an unfamiliar child, separation fear, and the reluctance to give up security objects all begin to decline in frequency and intensity around 2 years of age (Kagan, Kearsley, and Zelazo, 1978; Feldman and Ingham, 1975). Each of these phenomena results, in part, from response uncertainty that cannot be handled. The younger child does not have sturdy enough psychological functions to anticipate a source of uncertainty and prepare for it with some coping reaction. Awareness of the self's competences may fill this function.

This line of reasoning directy implies that when a child feels an obligation to meet standards set by others, she should show increased motivation to solve a variety of problems set by adults. Hence, quality of performance on adult-administered problems should improve. Most children showed improved performance on the memory task at about the same time they displayed distress to the model, and the occurrence of distress to the model—across the period 18–22 months in the younger cohort and 20–22 months in the older cohort—was correlated with the memory score at 22 months ($r = .67$, $p < .01$ for the younger cohort; $r = .46$, $p < .10$ for the older cohort).

The child should also try more conscientiously to simulate the examiner's drawing of a face. The 15-month-old may not realize that the face drawn by the examiner is a standard to be met and, therefore, does not try to draw a circle with internal elements. The 17-month-old is probably capable of putting a line or two inside the circle but may not because she does not yet completely appreciate the problem that has been posed and, more important, is not highly motivated to meet the standard set by the examiner.

If the 20-month-old is driven to meet standards, one would expect her language to approach adult form. The adult speech is the continual source of a standard that the child tries to match. She is not always successful because of cognitive limitations. Psycholinguists have tried to provide a detailed description of the course of perfectability. But the basic force originates in the inevitable and universal need to match one's products to standards extracted from adult behavior.

The recognition that one can meet self-generated or externally set goals provokes the desire to do so. A central quality of animal functioning is the disposition to perform what one is able to perform. Birds fly because they are capable of flying; children run because they can run. But what may be unique to the human species is the conscious decision to use competences one is aware of possessing. White has written that the two-year-old has a motive to be effective. We would add that, first, the 2-year-old must recognize she is effective.

The coherent set of studies implemented by Lewis and Brooks-Gunn (1979) are directly relevant to this work. They administered a variety of procedures to children 9 through 24 months of age in order to determine the time when these children showed signs of self-recognition. Their conclusion matches ours, for they found a major increase in behaviors indicative of recognition of self during the last half of the second year: "Between 18 and 21 months of age, a large increase in the number of infants demonstrating self-recognition abilities is seen across a wide range of representative modes . . . Clearly, self-recognition is well established by 21 months of age" (p. 215).

The most dramatic evidence favoring this conclusion involved the procedure originally reported by Gallup (1968) and Amsterdam (1972). Infants were first allowed to look at themselves in a mirror for approximately 90 seconds. Their noses were then unobtrusively marked with a spot of rouge, and they were brought back to the mirror to observe their reflection. A major variable of interest was the child's reaching for the place on his face where the mark of rouge had been put. Initially, when no rouge was on the face, no child under 21 months and only one 21-month-old and one 24-month-old touched their noses. With the rouge present, although no 9- or 12-month-old touched his nose, the tendency to do so rose dramatically from 15 to 24 months: over 60 percent of the 21- and 24-month-olds touched their noses. The individual variation in touching the nose and other indexes of self-recognition reported by Lewis and Brooks-Gunn were unrelated to the child's sex, number of siblings, or social class of family. The sharp increase in this behavior between 18 and 21 months suggests that the child's awareness of his own properties undergoes a major enhancement at this time. It cannot be a coincidence that this is the time when directives to adults, mastery smiles, and anxiety to the model also showed a sharp increase in frequency.

Changes in the play of the six children in Study 5 over the 10 months of observation suggest a slightly different and more speculative way of describing an essential facet of development during this interval. First, the child's behavior becomes generated from within rather than controlled from without. The 17-month-old plays with the toys in front of him and is easily distracted by a new toy or a sound of a truck outside. The 25-month-old selects objects he will play with and makes the objects accommodate to his ideas. He uses a truck as a telephone or a cup as a hat. The cup did not provoke the child to put it on his head. The child first had the idea and then looked for an appropriate object. The 2-year-old seems to be able to hold ideas—goals, plans, and action schemes—on the stage that philosophers call "consciousness" and psychologists call "awareness." She does not forget the ideas she generated.

One of the most striking changes in the child's play over the 10 months of observation was the increased duration of an episode of play. At 17 months the epochs of play that involved a particular object or theme lasted 10 to 15 seconds and were usually followed by an act that was theoretically independent of the one that preceded it. Subject L at 18½ months began the play session by closing a box. About 10 seconds later she put a toy telephone to her face, then gave a doll to the observer, and then pointed to the doll's feet. Each act seemed, on the surface, to be psychologically unrelated to its predecessor. But at 27 months L began the play session by picking up a doll and played with it for 12 minutes. She covered the doll, then picked it up and said, "Baby ready to get up," hugged the doll, covered it again, woke it, looked for an additional blanket, told the mother, "Don't touch her," declared again, "She's ready to get up," changed her diaper, played with the doll's eyes, took the cover off, and asked rhetorically, "Maybe she like a story?" Then she said, "Where's my story?" meaning, "Where is my storybook?" as if the word *story* elicited the idea of her own book. Such temporally extended sequences with one object and variations on the sleeping theme rarely occurred at 17 months.

Brenner and Mueller (1980) found a major increase in the duration of many social interaction sequences among groups of six boys observed over a 7-month period during the second year. This is the same era when children showed an increase in the duration of solitary play episodes, suggesting that a central change characteristic of this period of growth is the ability to sustain ideas and action plans. The psychological stage on which schemata interact and guide action does not collapse every half-minute or so. As a result, the child does not forget the goals he is pursuing, he asks his mother for help if he is unsuccessful, and he smiles upon attaining a self-generated goal. Perhaps what we have been calling self-awareness is better regarded as the capacity to hold cognitive representations on the stage of active memory. Maturing central nervous system structures and functions permit schemata to remain in consciousness for a longer period of time. This argument is appealing, because the available knowledge about the relation between brain function and psychological phenomena implies that damage to specific frontal and temporal areas of the brain is often accompanied by a loss of ability to retrieve past memories or to hold ideas on the stage that is called "active memory." Retrieval and maintenance of information seem to be yoked to central nervous system functioning in a fundamental way.

The suggestion that the enhancement of these behaviors is a consequence of brain growth finds persuasive support in data on histological changes in the young cerebral cortex. The length and degree of branching of dendrites in the human cerebral cortex do not approach adult magnitudes until 2 years of age; at birth, the dendritic pattern resembles that of the rat (Schadé and Ford, 1973). Additionally, during the second year there is an enhancement in the rate of myelination in association areas and intracortical plexuses (Lecours, 1975). Finally, Rabinowicz (1979) concluded that neuronal density (the number of neurons per unit volume) decreases very rapidly until birth: "From birth to between 3 and 6 months the decrease is slower and it ceases at about 15 months . . . one has to deduce that a very important moment in cortical maturation appears to be the period between 15 and 24 months, a period when almost all the layers reach, for the first time, a similar state of maturation" (p. 122). It may be no coincidence that this period corresponds to the interval when the child displays the behaviors that are regarded as indicative of self-awareness.

There are other examples, during the first two years of life, of correlations between signs of change in brain function and new psychological abilities. Dreyfus-Brisac (1979), who reviewed the data on brain bioelectrical activity, noted that at 3 months of age rhythmic activity (dominant frequency 3–4 cps) appears in the occipital area and is blocked with eye opening. Psychologists have noted that reliable habituation and dishabituation to a variety of events, as well as the first smiles to the human face, appear at this time. At 6 to 8 months of age a high amplitude theta rhythm (frequency 4 cps) appears during states of drowsiness. The period from 8 to 9 months is the age when object permanence, stranger and separation anxiety, avoidance of the visual cliff, and enhanced retrieval memory appear in most infants.

Although the psychological competences cannot appear until the brain has attained a certain level of maturity, the psychological functions are more than the new neural systems. We are not friendly to the extreme materialism of identity theory, which holds that all statements about behavior will eventually be reduced to sentences that contain only biological concepts. We are old-fashioned dualists with respect to the language used to explain psychological phenomena. When we say that a new behavior has matured we mean that an altered state of the central nervous system permitted a psychological incentive to provoke a new response.

All phenomena are part of a hierarchical arrangement where changes at one level are accompanied by changes at a markedly different level of description, owing to mysterious transformations whose mechanisms continue to evade interpretation. In that sense, self-awareness is not isomorphic with the central nervous system structures that permit it. As Sherrington noted, "That our being should consist of two fundamental elements offers, I suppose, no greater inherent improbability than that it should rest on one only" (in Penfield, 1975, p. 73).

There is a nice analogy in physics. If an accelerating electric charge (measured in velocity and energy) is placed in an electromagnetic field (measured in strength), a new phenomenon, radiation (measured in frequency), appears. The field is analogous to the state of the brain, the charge to an incentive stimulus, and the radiation to the behavioral event. Each of the phenomena in this trio is described in a different metric.

The hypothesis that awareness of standards and of the self's attributes is, in part, a psychological consequence of biological maturation may not be popular among some developmental psychologists. The popularity of any explanation—the feeling that an argument is valid —is a function of its accord with intuition and deductive rigor. Intuition refers to the unarticulated structures which take the form of tacit premises created from one's past experiences with that class of phenomena. If the articulated explanation offered by the scholar is in accord with these tacit suppositions, it will have strong intuitive appeal. Intuition is a common basis for persuasion in the social sciences because so many people hold beliefs about mind and behavior. The popularity of constructs like intelligence, anxiety, and identity derives from the fact that they give nominal status to less well-informed versions of these ideas. By contrast, explanations in sciences with a longer history and a richer intellectual corpus, like physics and chemistry, can have commanding power solely as a result of their deductive rigor. Steven Weinberg (1977) tried to describe what happened during the 3 minutes when the universe was first formed. A central conclusion in his argument is based on a single datum provided by the research of Wilson and Penzias (Penzias, 1979). That datum is the unexplained microwave radiation from the cosmos picked up by an antenna in Holmdel, New Jersey. By eliminating alternative explanations of this source of cosmic energy, the physicists concluded that it represented the energy that remained from the original creation of the universe about 20 billion years ago. I did not find this conclusion intuitively compelling. But apparently eminent physicists did, for Wilson and Penzias shared the Nobel Prize in 1978.

Why did a psychologist find this conclusion counterintuitive, while so many physicists did not? Of course, the physicist has a rich network of specialized facts I do not possess, which makes the conclusion intuitively more appealing to him than to me. But more important, the physicist is more prepared than the psychologist, psychiatrist, or parent to accept a conclusion that follows only from premises and facts arranged in a formal argument.

When a discipline does not have a large set of reliable facts, its practitioners tend to be suspicious of a rational argument, especially if the resulting conclusion violates intuition. In such disciplines, the appeal of an argument is determined largely by the tacit premises of the audience. Erik Erikson's (1950) writings have been popular with middle-class Americans because the nature of American life in urban and semiurban communities has made trust of a stranger, the ability to live alone, autonomous achievement, and identity central nodes of uncertainty. When a theorist articulates these concerns, his writing has the ring of validity.

The basic premise in developmental theory since World War I has been that the infant requires social interaction in order to develop the cognitive and affective qualities seen in later childhood. The differences among 3-year-olds in cognitive growth and behavioral profile are presumed to be a function of variation in social experiences. But theorists went one step further and suggested that the same forces which created the variation were also responsible for establishing the basic competence. Although variations in mother-child interactions can make one 2-year-old typically speak in five-word sentences and another in single words, it does not follow that these same events create the basic capacity for speech. This supposition implies that an infant who experiences no social interaction will not grow psychologically, despite Carmichael's (1927) demonstration that ambystoma, anesthetized until they were maturationally ready to swim, swam without prior practice, and Bühler's (1930) observations of swaddled Albanian children who quickly attained normative milestones when they were unbandaged. Additionally, Harlow (1966) found that a monkey raised in a black box did not fail to develop psychological dispositions, but the dispositions were markedly different from those of a nonisolate. Growth cannot be stopped, even in an environment where nothing physical is happening.

Relation to Traditional Views

If the changes we have described are inevitable psychological consequences of maturational events in the central nervous system, as long as the child lives in a world of objects and people, both current and traditional descriptions of the emergence of a sense of self may be misleading. Theorists in the psychoanalytic tradition, such as Mahler (1968), have assumed that initially the self was merged with another person and the infant gradually differentiated itself from the parent. But perhaps there is no self prior to the second year, as there is no frog in the tadpole and there are no morphemes hidden in the babbling of a 3-month-old.

The most popular view, supported by theorists with diverse agendas, insists that a sense of self develops, gradually, as a direct consequence of action. Preyer (1888) was reluctant to attribute the "I"-function only to endogenous changes in the central nervous system and, in agreement with the associationistic beliefs of his period, declared that it was through the child's actions and sense experiences that the "I"-feeling emerged: "Only by means of very frequent coincidences of unlike sense impressions, in tasting and touching, seeing and feeling, seeing and hearing, seeing and smelling, tasting and smelling, hearing and touching, are the intercentral connecting fibers developed, and then first can the various representational centers, these 'I'-makers, as it were, contribute, as in the case of the ordinary formation of concepts, to the formation of the corporate 'I,' which is quite abstract" (p. 205).

Guillaume (1926) suggested that the first phase of self was dependent upon imitation of others: "It is imitation that gradually causes the self to emerge from the unconscious" (p. 137). The pragmatist George Herbert Mead (1934) made social interaction a mandatory requirement for the first stage of self. The assimilation of others' attitudes to self, gained through active encounter, created the initial structure. Mead did not equivocate. The self "arises in the process of social experience and activity . . . It is impossible to conceive of a self arising outside of social experience" (pp. 135, 140).

Charles Cooley (1902) was closer to nineteenth century suppositions in awarding more influence to the perceptual and affective components of the self than to the action sector. Nonetheless, he too insisted that acts informing the young child of her effectiveness are prerequisites for the feeling of self, which "appears to be associated chiefly with ideas of the exercise of power and of being a cause" (p. 177). Piaget (1976) also stressed the relevance of interaction: "The subject only learns to know himself when acting on the object and the latter can become known only as the result of progress of the actions carried out on it" (p. 353).

Attempting to explain how Piagetian theory might inform language development, Sinclair-de-Zwart (1973) affirmed the three basic suppositions of Genevan theory—gradualism, interactionism, and connectivity. Knowledge develops slowly, requires interaction with persons and things, and advanced structures are reconstructions of previously acquired ones. However, it is not obvious that these ideas clarify the emergence of the child's directives to adults or self-descriptive utterances during the last half of the second year. Many investigators have tried, usually without success, to discover a relation between MLU, or other aspects of language, and performance on scales of sensory-motor functioning (Bloom et al., 1979). Additionally, commonalities that appear in the early speech of children are not totally consistent with Piaget's emphasis on interactions. The child manipulates the fingers and hair of her caretakers and herself, yet her first words for body parts rarely refer to these two elements but rather to the eyes, which do not participate in any manipulation. Leopold's (1939) daughter spoke as her first two words *pretty* and *de* (meaning "there" or "that"), rather than terms for the objects she played with most often. The salient phenomena of the second year do not seem to be easily derived from Piagetian theory.

Lewis and Brooks-Gunn (1979) also argued that the child's awareness of self, which grows parallel with her knowledge of others, "has as its source the interaction of the young organism with others—both people and objects . . . it is from action that knowledge develops" (p. 241), in a connected, stagelike sequence. Furthermore, "Social behavior—knowledge of the other, the self, and the relationship of the self to the other—is derived from early social reflexes" (p. 245). Although these psychologists did not explicitly deny that the maturation of a new competence lies at the root of self-recognition, they awarded to accumulated interactions with objects and people the major bases for the appearance of self-awareness and self-recognition.

Crook (1980) is unusual among modern theorists in his emphasis on cognitive maturation as an element in the emergence of consciousness: "The child's emerging sense of self is dependent upon the growth of its cognitive abilities in categorization, its experiences of contingency and agency in interaction with caregivers, and its experience of the emotional quality of its own conscious states" (p. 254).

I, too, believe that a child isolated from all people and objects will not develop self-awareness. But I am less certain that these processes and their attendant structures are necessarily created out of specific forms of feedback from imitation of others, play with parents, and the directing of adults. It is possible that the American children in Cambridge and Winston-Salem, the Fijians, and the Vietnamese refugees all displayed signs of apprehension to the modeling of acts during the last half of the second year because their patterns of social experience were similar. However, the remarkable temporal concordance for the appearance of distress to the model, across all samples, exceeded that for the onset of speech, which most scientists acknowledge depends in part on the maturation of new capacities. Perhaps no special class of social interaction is necessary for these competences to develop. Perhaps all that is required for the capacities called "self-awareness" to appear is any information resulting from the child's actions and feelings. The neurons of the visual cortex require patterned stimulation in order to mature and permit the psychological competence of discrimination. But almost any form of patterned stimulation will do. Similarly, certain species of birds living in isolated cages will sing their characteristic song at maturity if they only hear a tape-recorded version of it at the proper time; interaction with other birds is irrelevant. Obviously, social interaction contains a rich and complex source of information and probably hastens the development of these processes. But it is neither theoretically obvious nor empirically demonstrable that a child who has little or no material encounters with people will fail to develop the behaviors reflective of self-awareness, albeit at a slower rate. It is useful to take a strong skeptical stand, if only to stimulate relevant research.

The speculation that self-awareness is a direct consequence of a long history of material experiences with objects and people probably owes some of its popularity to the fact that most Western scholars have been reluctant to posit endogenous mechanisms, relatively independent of specific external experiences, which might be responsible for the emergence of new behaviors. During the opening decades of this century the naturalists in biology were generally opposed to the idea that spontaneous mutation in genes, rather than natural selection, was the major force in evolution. Similarly, many physiologists during most of the twentieth century have resisted the idea that the central nervous system does not necessarily require feedback from sense organs in order to generate coherent sequences of rhythmic movement during repetitive behavior, locomotion being the classic example. Most physiologists wanted to have sensory processes control basic movement patterns. But recent experimental evidence has led Delcomyn (1980) to argue persuasively that, "Isolation of the nervous system from all possible sources of sensory feedback does not abolish the normal pattern of rhythmic bursts in motoneurons . . . Timing of the repetitive movements that constitute any rhythmic behavior is regulated by intrinsic properties of the central nervous system rather than by sensory feedback from moving parts of the body" (p. 493).

Both physiologists and psychologists have wanted to believe that external events, potentially quantifiable, are the primary causes of action, because this premise is more in accord with an epistemology of mechanism and logical posivitism than with a presupposition that awards potency to entities which seem to have direction and structure from the beginning. The latter view leaves the investigator frustrated in his search for the chain of manipulable causes for the observed event.

Additionally, there is a deep prejudice against postulating significant entities that can arise with a short history. Western scientists prefer to impose gradualism on all instances of change. Thomas Henry Huxley warned Darwin that his insistence on gradual evolution represented "an unnecessary difficulty" in the theory, (in Gould 1980), and Gould argued that, on occasion, speciation can be rapid—a phenomenon he called "punctuated equilibria."

Increasingly sophisticated studies of morphological embryogenesis are verifying Weiss' (1968) suggestion that the differentiation of cells "produces a definite number of discrete, distinct, discontinuous and more or less sharply delimited cell types which are not connected by intergradations" (p. 212). Biologists now describe aspects of organ development in terms that explicitly assume abruptness of change. Newman and Frisch (1979) suggested that in the early formation of the chick limb there appear to be sudden structural changes. As a specific illustration, an enzyme (hyalurodinase) which inhibits precartilage cells from responding to a certain protein "makes its abrupt appearance in the developing chick limb immediately before the onset of chondrogenesis" (p. 664). The relatively discontinuous changes in the conditions surrounding the developing cartilage cells, rather than time, become the focal catalyst of growth: "it is not the amount of time spent by a population of cells in the subridge region that determines the proximo-distal character of the elements they will become part of" (p. 667). If the morphological growth of the embryo provides a useful model for early psychological growth, then a relatively sudden change in central nervous system function may be more important, for selected psychological competences, than the amount of time spent in a particular class of interactional experience. New developmental forms can occur, as D'Arcy Wentworth Thompson noted, without long periods of transition: "We cannot transform an invertebrate into a vertebrate nor a coelenterate into a worm by any single and legitimate deformation . . . Nature proceeds from one type to another . . . To seek for steppingstones across the gaps between is to seek in vain forever" (in Gould, 1980, p. 193).

Problem of Transition

The gradualness—or suddenness—of developmental changes cannot be determined without first deciding on the mechanisms of change. This issue remains obscure. Indeed, the central lacuna in most developmental theories is the absence of well-articulated mechanisms that explain transition. Consider a mechanism that conveys some degree of understanding. Physiologists assert that changes in the hypothalamus and pituitary at puberty lead to the release of hormones, which in turn produce alterations in morphology. Even though scientists cannot state what mechanisms lead to the altered functioning of the hypothalamus and pituitary, their data clarify the causes of the growth of primary and secondary sexual characteristics.

Two major classes of mechanisms are postulated to interpret psychological change. The most popular assumes that a structure, or process, gradually becomes enhanced until it reaches a critical magnitude. As a consequence, the entity is transformed and a new surface phenomenon emerges, as a growing seed pod suddenly bursts when it becomes too full. One psychological example of this class of change is contained in the popular suggestion that a cognitive structure becomes accessible to report as a result of increasing articulation of the structure through repeated experience. This mechanism, which might be called "change through enhancement," is the central process in learning theory explanations of behavioral development, and one that preserves continuity and gradualism.

In a second, more complex instance of change, the new form emerges as a result of the introduction of a new function. Although the new form is often dependent on earlier structures, it could not have resulted from enhancement. The new form required either the maturation of a new process or an encounter with a new set of experiences. The onset of spoken language provides an example of the first type. The child cannot speak meaningful utterances until he first understands some words. But most scholars assume some special function has to be added if the child is to talk. We typically postulate an endogenous change in the central nervous system—the growth of a neurological mechanism—which permits the child to utilize his linguistic knowledge. It would not occur simply as a result of increasingly sophisticated comprehension. This class of change is called "endogenous" in order to imply that a novel function had to be introduced. As with enhancement, however, the new form could have been dependent on earlier functions. There is a great deal of resistance to assuming that the maturation of central nervous system functions, in contrast to special experiences, is necessary for the appearance of new psychological phenomena. Some psychologists write as if all novel functions were a product of gradual enhancement. But when a new form replaces an old one (as when speech replaces gestures) or when an old form simply disappears (as in the Moro reflex), it is difficult to avoid positing the introduction of a new function that replaces or inhibits the older one.

The mechanisms that are presently used to explain change in cognitive structure or process include the concept of accommodation, Piaget's major force for change. Most psychologists agree with the spirit of Piaget's claim that in the process of accommodating to new events, cognitive structures are altered. Consider an infant's schema for her mother's face. If the child notes a discrepancy from her schema—a new hat, scarf, or scar—and accommodates to the new feature, an alteration of the original structure will occur. Observation of young children suggests that this mechanism is an inherent property of the mind. Children habitually note discrepancies from their schemata and, on occasion, alter existing schemata so that they are in accord with a discrepant event.

Finally, the child creates changes in units through her own thought. The child compares two sequences of knowledge, notes an inconsistency, and makes a change in one or both. The incentive for change is the detection of variation between knowledge and new events. But principles are needed to specify which variations will be most effective in generating change. The unsolved problem, and the node of controversy, is determination of the balance betweeen the psychological sequelae of autochthonous central nervous system changes and those of experience in generating changes in cognitive function and the construction of new organizations. Most psychologists acknowledge that cognitive units are continually undergoing change because the child is continually detecting variation. But at times the introduction of new processes leads to qualitative changes in function which cannot be predicted or derived from assessing the continual operation of assimilation, accommodation, and equilibration following encounter with new experiences. Perhaps the new synthesis in developmental psychology, like the recent synthesis in evolutionary biology, will result from a unification of the maturational and experiential contributions to psychological growth.

Concept of Consciousness

The compelling nature of consciousness as a phenomenon, together with its recalcitrance to analysis, have made it a popular theme among Western philosophers and modern neurophysiologists, both of whom have chosen consciousness over sleep, anger, or the ability to thread a needle as the primary intellectual challenge. Most nineteenth century observers distinguished between a sense of self, which they agreed appeared in the second year, and the first signs of consciousness, which emerged in the form of will at the end of the first year. No major text on children written from 1880 to 1900 failed to treat the construct of will, and most writers were in consensus as to its meaning.

Will was the inner force responsible for voluntary action. Very young infants could not have a will, even though they displayed movement, because they did not have volitional control of those movements. According to Preyer (1888), "Every willed movement is preceded directly by ideas, one of which, finally as cause of the movement, acquires motor force" (p. 193). The will was not "inborn" but "hereditary" (p. 194), and Preyer dated the reliable emergence of will at 7 to 8 months of age when the first volitional imitation occurred.

Modern scholars have been less concerned with when consciousness emerged than with its biological basis, and whether its experiential core is universal or socially constructed. The infant's behavior during the first 8 months does not require a term implying consciousness. The only phenomenon which comes close to that demand is recognition memory, the infant's tendency to look less at event A than event B if 10 minutes earlier he saw event A for one minute. It is necessary to posit some psychological function that recognizes event A the second time. In order to avoid terms with misleading connotations, we call it the REC function. The REC function relates external events in the field to a schema. Bacteria also relate a quality of certain sugars in the external environment to internal structures, and it does not seem necessary to posit consciousness to explain the fact that these single-celled forms move toward the sugar that was present in their rearing environment.

The next two functions to emerge are the retrieval of schemata without any cues in the immediate field and the generation of inferences following the relating of those schemata to present experience. When a 14-month-old searches persistently for a particular toy she saw hidden 30 seconds earlier, behaving as if she knows it must be somewhere, it is assumed that she retrieves and maintains a schemata for the earlier hiding and generates an inference about the existence of the toy. Let us call these functions RET, meaning retrieval of the past and relating it to the present, and INF, meaning inference. Thus, by the middle of the second year the child has acquired three functions—REC, RET, and INF. Although they are not automatic, they do not require the positing of a function that monitors, initiates and terminates them. This process emerges after 16 or 17 months when the child becomes aware of her ability to select and control actions. We call this process AW, meaning awareness of one's potentiality for action. This function comes closest to what has been called consciousness.

The fifth competence to appear, which is not completely explained by the four functions already postulated, is an awareness of the self as an entity with attributes. To explain why a 30-month-old declares, laughingly, "I'm a baby," as she crawls on the floor and sucks on a bottle, requires more than an awareness of one's ability to act. This behavior presupposes not only a schema for one's actions but also a schema for the self as an object with variations in attributes. So we posit finally an awareness of self as an entity with characteristics, which we call SF. The sequence from REC through RET, INF, AW, and SF represents an enhancement of control, selection, and awareness, just as the increasing encephalization that accompanies phylogeny results in an enhanced integration of subordinate functions.

The degree of connectedness among these five functions is obscure. Although the first four are all presumed by SF (SF could not exist without them), SF need not emerge from them. That is, SF is not an inevitable process; some new processes must be inserted into the developmental sequence if SF is to appear. Once again we encounter the ancient enigma in historical sequence. What propositions must we invent to describe how novel properties use and subsume earlier ones, but are not produced by them? The biologist who wishes to explain morphological changes in phylogeny faces the same problem. The convolutions of the cerebral cortex depend on the prior existence of a forebrain. But without the mutations that were a part of evolution, no convolutions would have occurred. Unique endogenous changes are required if the novel structure is to appear. REC, RET, INF, and AW are necessary for SF, but not sufficient. To recognize, retrieve, infer, and know what one can do, how one feels, and how one is similar to and different from another represent sequentially ordered events in the growth of consciousness. The half-dozen months from the first smile following completion of a block tower to the declaration, "I can't do that," contain one of the most significant sets of competences that appear in our species.

References
Index

References

Amsterdam, B. K. Mirror Self-Image Reactions Before Age Two. *Developmental Psychology* 5 (1972): 297–305.

Arlitt, A. H. *Psychology of Infancy and Early Childhood.* New York: McGraw-Hill, 1928.

Baldwin, J. M. *Mental Development in the Child and the Race.* New York: Macmillan, 1895.

———. *Social and Ethical Interpretations in Mental Development.* New York: Macmillan, 1897.

Bandura, A. *Social Learning Theory.* Englewood Cliffs, N.J.: Prentice Hall, 1977.

Benedict, H. Early Lexical Development. *Journal of Child Language* 6 (1979): 183–200.

Bernfeld, S. *The Psychology of the Infant.* New York: Brentano's, 1929.

Bierwisch, M. Some Semantic Universals of German Adjectivals. *Foundations of Language* 3 (1967): 1–36.

Bloom, L. *Language Development: Form and Function in Emerging Grammars.* Cambridge: MIT Press, 1970.

———. *One Word at a Time: The Use of Single Word Utterances Before Syntax.* The Hague: Mouton, 1973.

Bloom, L.; Lifter, K.; and Broughton, J. What Children Say and What They Know. Paper delivered at Conference on Language Development, Santa Barbara, Cal., Oct. 11–13, 1979.

Bloom, L.; Lifter, K.; and Hafitz, J. Semantics of Verbs and the Development of Verb Inflection in Child Language. *Language* 56 (1980): 386–412.

Bloom, L.; Lightbown, P.; and Hood, L. Structure and Variation in Child Language. *Monographs of the Society for Research in Child Development* 40, no. 2 (1975): 1–97.

Bloom, L., Miller, P., Hood, L. Variation and Reduction as Aspects of Competence in Language Development. In A. Pick, ed. *Minnesota Symposium on Child Psychology.* Vol. 9. Minneapolis: University of Minnesota Press, 1975, pp. 3–51.

Bowerman, M. *Early Syntactic Development: A Cross Linguistic Study with Special Reference to Finnish.* Cambridge: Cambridge University Press, 1973.

———. Structural Relationships in Children's Utterances: Syntactic or Semantic? In T. E. Moore, ed. *Cognitive Development and the Acquisition of Language.* New York: Academic Press, 1973, pp. 197–213.

Braine, M. D. S. Length Constraints, Reduction Rules, and Holophrastic Process in Children's Word Combinations. *Journal of Verbal Learning and Verbal Behavior* 13 (1974): 448–456.

Breland, K., and Breland, M. The Misbehavior of Organisms. *American Psychologist* 16 (1960): 661–664.

Brenner, J., and Mueller, E. Shared Meaning in Boy Toddler Peer Relations. Unpublished manuscript, Boston University, 1980.

Bretherton, I.; McNew, S.; and Beeghly-Smith, M. Early Person Knowledge as Expressed in Gestural and Verbal Communications. In M. E. Lamb and L. R. Sherrod, eds. *Infant Social Cognition*. Hillsdale, N.J.: Erlbaum Associates, 1981, pp. 333–377.

Bridgman, P. W. Determinism in Modern Science. In S. Hook, ed. *Determinism and Freedom in the Age of Modern Science*. New York: New York University Press, 1958, pp. 43–63.

Briggs, J. L. *Never in Anger*. Cambridge: Harvard University Press, 1970.

Brown, R. *A First Language: The Early Stages*. Cambridge: Harvard University Press, 1973.

Bühler, C. *The First Year of Life*. New York: John Day, 1930 (rprt. New York: Arno, 1975).

———. *From Birth to Maturity*. London: Kegan, Paul, Trench, Trubner, 1935.

Carmichael, L. A Further Study of the Development of Behavior in Vertebrates Experimentally Removed from the Influence of External Stimulation. *Psychological Review* 34 (1927): 34–47.

Clark, E. V. What's in a Word: On the Child's Acquisition of Semantics in His First Language. In T. E. Moore, ed. *Cognitive Development and the Acquisition of Language*. New York: Academic Press, 1973, pp. 65–110.

———. Awareness of Language: Some Evidence from What Children Say and Do. In A. Sinclair, R. J. Jarvella, and W. J. M. Levelt, eds. *The Child's Conception of Language*. New York: Springer Verlag, 1978, pp. 17–43.

———. Building a Vocabulary. In P. Fletcher and M. Garmon, eds. *Language Acquisition*. New York: Cambridge University Press, 1979, pp. 149–160.

Clark, E. V., and Anderson, E. S. Spontaneous Repairs: Awareness in the Progress of Acquiring Language. Paper presented at a meeting of the Society for Research in Child Development, San Francisco, Cal., Mar. 15–19, 1979.

Cooley, C. H. *Human Nature and the Social Order*. New York: Charles Scribners, 1902.

———. *Social Organization*. New York: Charles Scribners, 1909.

Cromer, R. The Development of Language and Cognition: The Cognitive Hypothesis. In B. Foss, ed. *New Perspectives in Child Development*. New York: Penquin, 1974, pp. 184–252.

Crook, J. H. *The Evolution of Human Consciousness*. Oxford: Clarendon Press, 1980.

Darwin, C. *Descent of Man and Selection in Relation to Sex*. Vol. 1. New York: D. Appleton, 1871.

Davis, W. A., and Havighurst, R. J. *The Father of the Man*. Boston: Houghton-Mifflin, 1947.

Delcomyn, F. Neural Bases of Rhythmic Behavior in Animals. *Science* 210 (1980): 492–498.

D'Espagnat, B. The Quantum Theory and Relativity. *Scientific American* 241, no. 5 (1979): 158–181.

Donaldson, H. H. *The Growth of the Brain.* London: Walter Scott, 1895.

Dreyfus-Brisac, C. Ontogenesis of Brain Bio-electrical Activity and Sleep Organization in Neonates and Infants. In F. Falkner and J. M. Tanner, eds. *Human Growth.* Vol. 3. New York: Plenum, 1979, pp. 157–182.

Eckerman, C. O.; Whatley, J. L.; and Kutz, S. L. Growth of Social Play with Peers During the Second Year of Life. *Developmental Psychology* 11 (1975): 42–49.

Eddington, A. S. *The Nature of the Physical World.* Cambridge: Cambridge University Press, 1928.

Erikson, E. H. *Childhood and Society.* New York: Norton, 1950.

Feldman, S. S., and Ingham, M. E. Attachment Behavior: A Validation Study in Two Age Groups. *Child Development* 46 (1975): 319–330.

Fenson, L., and Ramsay, D. S. Decentration and Integration of the Child's Play in the Second Year. *Child Development* 51 (1980): 171–178.

Ferguson, C. A. Baby Talk in Six Languages. *American Anthropologist* 66 (1964): 103–114.

Ferguson, G. O. The Psychology of the Negro. *Archives of Psychology* 36 (1916): 100–130.

Fischer, K. W., and Corrigan, R. Skill Approach to Language Development. Paper delivered at Conference on Language Development, Santa Barbara, Cal., Oct. 11–13, 1979.

Gallup, G. G. Mirror Image Stimulation. *Psychological Bulletin* 70 (1968): 782–793.

Garcia, J., and Koelling, R. Relation of Cue to Consequence in Avoidance Learning. *Psychonomic Science* 4 (1966): 123–124.

Gelman, R. Cognitive Development. In M. R. Rosenzweig and L. W. Porter, eds. *Annual Review of Psychology.* Vol. 29. Palo Alto, Cal.: Annual Reviews, 1978, pp. 297–332.

Gentner, D. On Relational Meaning: The Acquisition of Verb Meaning. *Child Development* 49 (1978): 988–998.

Globus, G. G.; Maxwell, G.; and Savodnik, I., eds. *Consciousness and the Brain.* New York: Plenum, 1976.

Goldin-Meadow, S.; Seligman, M. E. P.; and Gelman, R. Language in the Two-Year-old. *Cognition* 4 (1976): 189–202.

Gorer, G. Theoretical Approaches, 1941. In M. Mead and M. Wolfenstein, eds. *Children in Contemporary Cultures.* Chicago: University of Chicago Press, 1955, pp. 31–36.

Gould, S. J. *The Panda's Thumb.* New York: W. W. Norton, 1980.

Greenfield, P. M. Informativeness, Presupposition and Semantic Choice in Single-Word Utterances. In E. Ochs and B. B. Schiefflin, eds. *Developmental Pragmatics.* New York: Academic Press, 1979, pp. 159–166.

Greenfield, P. M., and Smith, J. H. *The Structure of Communication and the Beginnings of Language Development.* New York: Academic Press, 1976.

Greenfield, P. M., and Zukow, P. G. Why Children Say What They Say When They Say It. In K. E. Nelson, ed. *Children's Language*. Vol. 1. New York: Gardner Press, 1978, pp. 287–336.

Griffin, D. R. *The Question of Animal Awareness*. New York: The Rockefeller University Press, 1976.

Guillaume, P. *Imitation in Children*. Trans. E. D. Halperin, Chicago: University of Chicago Press, 1971 (Paris: Press Universitaires de France, 1926).

Hanson, N. R. *Patterns of Discovery*. Cambridge: Cambridge University Press, 1961.

Harlow, H. F., and Harlow, M. H. Learning to Love. *American Scientist* 54 (1966): 244–272.

Harnick, F. S. The Relationship Between Ability Level and Task Difficulty in Producing Imitation in Infants. *Child Development* 49 (1978): 209–212.

Hay, D. F. Cooperative Interactions and Sharing Between Very Young Children and Their Parents. *Developmental Psychology* 15 (1979): 647–653.

Hetherington, E. M., and Parke, R. D. *Child Psychology*. 2nd ed. New York: McGraw-Hill, 1979.

Holmberg, M. C. The Development of Social Interchange Patterns from 12 to 42 Months. *Child Development* 51 (1980): 448–456.

Huntington, D. S. Supportive Programs for Infants and Parents. In J. Osofsky, ed. *Handbook of Infant Development*. New York: John Wiley, 1979, pp. 837–851.

Hurlock, E. *Developmental Psychology*. 4th ed. New York: McGraw-Hill, 1975.

Kagan, J. *Change and Continuity in Infancy*. New York: John Wiley, 1971.

Kagan, J. The Form of Early Development. *Archives of General Psychiatry* 36 (1979a): 1047–1054.

Kagan, J. Overview: Perspectives on Human Infancy. In J. Osofsky, ed. *Handbook of Infant Development*. New York: John Wiley, 1979b, pp. 1–28.

Kagan, J. Perspectives on Continuity. In O. G. Brim and J. Kagan, eds. *Constancy and Change in Human Development*. Cambridge: Harvard University Press, 1980, pp. 26–74.

Kagan, J.; Kearsley, R. B.; and Zelazo, P. R. *Infancy: Its Place in Human Development*. Cambridge: Harvard University Press, 1978.

Kagan, J.; Linn, S.; Mount, R.; Reznick, J. S.; and Hiatt, S. Asymmetry of Inference in the Dishabituation Paradigm. *Canadian Journal of Psychology* 33 (1979): 288–305.

Kagan, J., and Moss, H. A. *Birth to Maturity*. New York: John Wiley, 1962.

Katz, M. M. W. Gaining Sense at Age Two in the Outer Fiji Islands. Unpublished doctoral dissertation, Harvard Graduate School of Education, 1981.

King, I. *The Psychology of Child Development*. Chicago: Chicago University Press, 1907.

Koffka, K. *Growth of the Mind*. New York: Harcourt-Brace, 1924.

Land, P. W., and Lund, R. D. Development of the Rat's Uncrossed Retino-

Tectal Pathway and Its Relation to Plasticity Studies. *Science* 205 (1979): 698–700.

Largo, R. H., and Howard, J. A. Developmental Progression in Play Behavior of Children Between 9 and 30 Months. *Developmental Medicine and Child Neurology* 1–2, no. 21 (1979): 299–310, 492–503.

Lecours, A. R. Myelogenetic Correlates of the Development of Speech and Language. In E. H. Lenneberg and E. Lenneberg, eds. *Foundations of Language Development*. Vol. 1. New York: Academic Press, 1975, pp. 121–135.

Leopold, W. F. *Speech Development of a Bilingual Child*. Vol. 1. Evanston: Northwestern University Press, 1939.

Lewis, M., and Brooks-Gunn, J. *Social Cognition and the Acquisition of Self*. New York: Plenum, 1979.

Locke, J. *An Essay Concerning Human Understanding* (1690). Philadelphia: T. Ellwood Zell, 1898.

Lowe, M. Trends in the Development of Representational Play in Infants from One to Three Years. *Journal of Child Psychology and Psychiatry* 16 (1975): 33–47.

Luria, A. R. *Cognitive Development: Its Cultural and Social Foundations*. Ed. M. Cole. Cambridge, Mass.: Harvard University Press, 1976.

Macnamara, J. Cognitive Basis for Language Learning in Infants. *Psychological Review* 79 (1972): 1–13.

Mahler, M. S. *On Human Symbiosis and the Vicissitudes of Individuation*. Vol. 1. *Infantile Psychosis*. New York: International University Press, 1968.

Mandelbaum, M. *History, Man and Reason*. Baltimore: The Johns Hopkins University Press, 1971.

Marwedel, E. *Conscious Motherhood*. Part 1. Boston: D. C. Heath, 1889.

Matheny, A. P. Bayley's Infant Behavior Record: Behavioral Components and Twin Analyses. *Child Development* 51 (1980): 1157–1167.

Maurice, F. D. *The Life and Letters of F. D. Maurice*. Vol. 1 *1884*. 4th ed. London: Macmillan, 1885.

May, H. S. *The End of American Innocence*. New York: Knopf, 1959.

McCall, R. B.; Parke, R. D.; and Kavanaugh, R. D. Imitation of Live and Televised Model by Children One to Three Years of Age. *Monographs of the Society for Research in Child Development* 42, no. 5 (1977): 1–94.

McKenzie, B. E.; Tootell, H. E.; and Day, R. H. Development of Visual Size Constancy During the First Year of Human Infancy. *Developmental Psychology* 16 (1980): 163–174.

McNeill, D. *The Acquisition of Language*. New York: Harper, 1970.

———. The Capacity for the Ontogenesis of Grammar. In D. I. Slobin, ed. *The Ontogenesis of Grammar*. New York: Academic Press, 1971, pp. 17–40.

Mead, G. H. *Mind, Self, and Society*. Chicago: University of Chicago Press, 1934.

Merry, F. K., and Merry, R. V. *The First Two Decades of Life: A Revision and Extension of from Infancy to Adolescence*. New York: Harper & Row, 1950.

Moore, M.; Kagan, J.; and Sahl, M. Retrieval and Evaluation in Reading Disability. *Bulletin of the Orton Society* (in press).

Moruzzi, G., and Magoun, H. W. Brain Stem Reticular Formation and Activation of the EEG. *Electroencephalography and Clinical Neurophysiology* 1 (1949): 455–473.

Mumford, E. E. R. *The Dawn of Character in the Mind of the Child.* New York: Longmans Green, 1925.

Mussen, P. H.; Conger, J. J.; and Kagan, J. *Child Development and Personality.* 3rd ed. New York: Harper & Row, 1969.

Mussen, P. H.; Conger, J. J.; and Kagan, J. *Child Development and Personality.* 4th ed. New York: Harper & Row, 1974.

Nelson, K. Structure and Strategy in Learning to Talk. *Monographs of the Society for the Research in Child Development* 38, serial no. 149 (1973).
———. Concept, Word and Sentence: Interrelations in Acquisition and Development. *Psychological Review* 81 (1974): 267–285.
———. Some Attributes of Adjectives Used byYoung Children. *Cognition* 4 (1976): 13–30.

Nelson, K. E., and Bonvillian, J. D. Concepts and Words in the Eighteen-Month-Old. *Cognition* 2 (1973): 435–450.

Newman, S. A., and Frisch, H. L. Dynamics of Skeletal Pattern Formation in Developing Chick Limb. *Science* 205 (1979): 662–668.

Nicolich, L. M. Beyond Sensorimotor Intelligence: Assessment of Symbolic Maturity Through Analysis of Pretend Play. *Merrill-Palmer Quarterly* 23 (1977): 90–99.

Norsworthy, N., and Whitley, M. T. *Psychology of Childhood.* Rev. ed. New York: Macmillan, 1933.

Novey, M. S. The Development of Knowledge of Others' Ability to See. Unpublished doctoral dissertation, Harvard University, 1975.

Osofsky, J. D. *Handbook of Infant Development.* New York: Wiley, 1979.

Penfield, W. *The Mystery of the Mind.* Princeton: Princeton University Press, 1975.

Penzias, A. A. The Origin of the Elements. *Science* 205 (1979): 549–554.

Perez, B. *The First Three Years of Childhood.* Trans. A. M. Christie. London: Swann Sonnenchein, 1900.

Piagét, J. *Play, Dreams and Imitation in Childhood.* Trans. C. Gattegno and F. M. Hodgson. London: Routledge and Kegan Paul, 1951.
———. *The Grasp of Consciousness.* Cambridge: Harvard University Press, 1976.

Pinchbeck, I., and Hewitt, M. *Children in English Society.* Vols. 1–2. London: Routledge and Kegan Paul, 1969, 1973.

Preyer, W. *The Mind of the Child.* Part 1. *The Senses and the Will.* New York: D. Appleton, 1888.
———. *The Mind of the Child.* Part 2. *The Development of Intellect.* New York: D. Appleton, 1889.

Rabinowicz, T. The Differentiate Maturation of the Human Cerebral Cortex. In F. Falkner and J. M. Tanner, eds. *Human Growth.* Vol. 3. New York: Plenum, 1979, pp. 97–123.

Rader, N.; Bausano, M.; and Richards, J. E. On the Nature of the Visual-Cliff Avoidance Response in Human Infants. *Child Development* 51 (1980): 61–68.

Rand, W.; Sweeny, M. E.; and Vincent, E. L. *Growth and Development of the Young Child.* Philadelphia: W. B. Saunders, 1930.

Ricciuti, H. N. Object Grouping and Selective Ordering Behavior in Infants Twelve to Twenty-Four Months Old. *Merrill-Palmer Quarterly of Behavior and Development* 11 (1965): 129–148.

Rodgon, M. M.; Jankowski, W.; and Alenskas, L. A Multi-functional Approach to Single-Word Usage. *Journal of Child Language* 4 (1977): 23–43.

Rogoff, B. A Study of Memory in a Highland Maya Society. Unpublished doctoral dissertation, Harvard University, 1978.

Romanes, G. J. *Mental Evolution in Man.* New York: D. Appleton, 1889 (reprt. New York: Arno, 1975).

Schadé, J. P., and Ford, D. H. *Basic Neurology.* 2nd ed. Amsterdam: Elsevier, 1973.

Schlesinger, I. M. Production of Utterances and Language Acquisition. In D. I. Slobin, ed. *The Ontogenesis of Grammar.* New York: Academic Press, 1971, pp. 63–102.

———. Relational Concepts Underlying Language. In R. L. Schiefelbush and L. L. Lloyd, eds. *Language Perspectives: Acquisition, Retardation, and Intervention.* Baltimore: University Park Press, 1974, pp. 129–152.

Sellers, M. J. G. *The Enhancement of Memory in Costa Rican Children.* Unpublished doctoral dissertation, Harvard University, 1979.

Shinn, M. *Notes on the Development of a Child.* (Berkeley: University of California Publications in Education, 1907).

Sinclair-de-Zwart, H. Language Acquisition and Cognitive Development. In T. E. Moore, ed. *Cognitive Development and the Acquisition of Language.* New York: Academic Press, 1973, pp. 9–25.

Slobin, D. I. Language Change in Childhood and History. In J. Macnamara, ed. *Language, Learning and Thought.* New York: Academic Press, 1977, pp. 185–214.

Spemann, H., and Mangold, H. Ueber Induktion von Embryonalanlogen durch Implantation artfrender Organisatoren. *Archives Mikroskop. Anat. u. Entwicklungsmech* 100 (1924): 599–638.

Stern, C., and Stern, W. *Die Kindersprache: Eine Psychologische und Sprachtheoritische untersuchwag.* 4th ed. Leipzig: Barth, 1928.

Stern, W. *Psychology of Early Chidhood.* trans. A. Barwell. 6th ed. New York: Henry Holt, 1930.

Sully, J. Studies of Childhood. New York: D. Appleton, 1896.

Terman, L. M. *The Measurement of Intelligence.* Boston: Houghton Mifflin, 1916.

Tiedemann, D. *Beobachtungen über die Entwicklung der Seelenfähigkeiten.* 1st ed., 1787. Altenburg: Oskar Bonde, 1897.

Tracy, F., and Stimpfl, J. *The Psychology of Childhood.* 7th ed. Boston: D. C. Heath, 1909.

Tylor, E. B. *Researches into the Early History of Mankind.* New York: Holt, 1878.

Wachs, T. P., and Hubert, N. C. Changes in the Structure of Cognitive Intellectual Performance During the Second Year of Life. *Infant Behavior and Development.* In press.

Watson, J. Psychological Care of Infant and Child. New York: Norton, 1928.

Weinberg, S. *The First Three Minutes*. New York: Basic Books, 1977.

Weiskrantz, L. Trying to Bridge Some Neuropsychological Gaps Between Monkey and Man. *British Journal of Psychology* 68 (1977): . 431–445.

Weiss, P. A. *Dynamics of Development*. New York: Academic Press, 1968.

White, R. W. Motivation Reconsidered: The Concept of Competence. *Psychological Review* 66 (1959): 297–333.

Wooten, J.; Merkin, S.; Hood, L.; and Bloom, L. *Wh*. Questions: Linguistic Evidence to Explain the Sequence of Acquisition. Paper presented at a meeting of the Society for Research in Child Development, San Francisco, Cal., Mar. 15–19, 1979.

Yando, R.; Seitz, V.; and Zigler, E. *Imitation: A Developmental Perspective*. Hillsdale, N.J.: L. Erlbaum, 1978.

Yerkes, R. M. *Psychological Examining in the United States Army*. Memoirs of the National Academy of Sciences, vol. 15. Washington, D.C.: National Academy of Sciences, 1921.

Index